Training for ELECTED PANCHAYATI RAJ REPRESENTATIVES

Training for
Elected Panchayati Raj Representatives

R.K. Tiwari

SHIPRA

ISBN: 978-81-7541-412-9

First Published in India in 2008

Training for
Elected Panchayati Raj Representatives

Published by:
SHIPRA PUBLICATIONS
115-A, Vikas Marg, Shakarpur
Delhi - 110092 (India)
Ph.: 91-11-65277210, 22500954; Fax : 22458662;
Email: info@shiprapublications.com
www.shiprapublications.com

Dedicated to the memory of my sister
Dr. Anita Sharma

Foreword

The emergence of local representative bodies since 1882 marked a distinct phase in the evolution of these institutions in India. Prior to 1882, such institutions were based on the caste factor and the prevailing social order. Besides, these were not sponsored by the state. An attempt was made by Lord Mayo, prior to Lord Ripon, in the setting up of local representative bodies. Constitutional developments in Britain during that period also influenced the evolution of local representative bodies in India. John Stuart Mill in his writings provided distinct role, responsibilities as well as an obligation on the state to provide political education to the masses through the instrumentally of local bodies. Political education was the principal reason for the emergence of local representative institutions during the British period of India. These institutions played a very significant role in the political awakening of the country. The most illustrious of our leaders in the freedom movement played an important role in the development of these institutions, particularly in the field of urban local government.

The debate and discussion and widely differing viewpoints regarding Panchayati Raj in the Constituent Assembly are well known. There was no specific mention regarding the place of village panchayats in the Resolution on the Aims and Objectives of India's Constitution introduced in the Constituent Assembly on 13th December 1946. In an article in *Harijan* on 21st December 1947, Gandhiji observed "I must confess that I have not been able to follow the proceedings of the Constituent

Assembly..(the correspondent) says that there is no mention or direction about village panchayats and decentralization in the foreshadowed Constitution. It is certainly an omission calling for immediate attention if our independence is to reflect the peoples' voice. The greater the power of the panchayats, the better for the people..." Besides, several speakers in the Constituent Assembly also made a reference to a statement of Gandhiji where he said: "The centre of power now is in New Delhi, or in Calcutta and Bombay, in the big cities. I would have it distributed among the seven hundred thousand villages of India..." This led to the inclusion of Article 40 as a part of the Directive Principles of State Policy. However, it was soon realized in the course of planning process as observed by Balvantray Mehta Committee that it is difficult to envisage development without the participation of the people. The First Prime Minister of India, Pandit Jawaharlal Nehru, more than any one else, supported the idea of decentralized democracy. I distinctly recall some of his 'Annual Addresses' (1954-1963) as the President of the Indian Institute of Public Administration (IIPA) where he spoke of the need for these institutions. He was in favour of giving importance to panchayats. He was keen that these institutions should not be dominated by officials. The official element should act primarily as advisors. He was all in favour of panchayat members making mistakes and learning from them. He was keen that every attention should be given to administrative problems of panchayats so as to strengthen them.

The Asoka Mehta Committee (1978) examined the functioning of Panchayati Raj Institutions (PRIs) and observed that these institutions were being dominated by the economically and socially privileged classes and benefits were also being cornered by them. The Committee also stressed the need for providing a constitutional base for these institutions. The emergence of rural development with a focus on poverty alleviation again highlighted the need for rejuvenating the PRIs. Many scholarly publications and the government reports again stressed the need for appropriate people's institutions at the district level and below. The G.V.K. Rao Committee Report

(1985) and L.M. Singhvi's concept paper (1986) highlighted the importance of PRIs as vehicles of social and economic transformation. Efforts were made through the 64th (1989) and 69th (1990) Constitutional Amendment Bills to achieve the above objectives.

The task of empowering the PRIs and providing a constitutional base was ensured through the Constitution (Seventy-third) Amendment Act, 1992. This amendment was historic, as it accorded constitutional status to these bodies along with the provision for regular elections, Constitution of State Election Commissions, and State Finance Commissions, reservation for Scheduled Castes, and Scheduled Tribes, according to their population and 33 per cent reservation for women. Equally important is the place accorded to Gram Sabha in the overall structure of these institutions. The working of these institutions over the last 10 years has brought out again that lack of awareness of their proper role and responsibilities, besides sway of parochial considerations, at least at the level of village panchayat and also intermediate panchayat tend to hamper the effective functioning of these institutions.

Training of approximately three million elected representatives of Panchayati Raj is a difficult and complex task. Training, if properly conceived and planned, could play an important role in strengthening and empowering the elected representatives. All the more, it is needed as a large number of elected representatives belong to the Scheduled Castes, Scheduled Tribes and women. They have to be imparted confidence and knowledge about their role and responsibilities. The training programme should be conceived at all the levels on a continuous basis in a decentralized manner. Without training, it is difficult for elected representatives to understand the complexities involved in the administrative and financial processes of the Panchayati Raj system. The development schemes and their broad guidelines regarding the financial and administrative parameters are also important. It will help in making them articulate and knowledgeable.

Unfortunately, the training aspect has remained neglected. The experience gathered during the Community Development programme and the first phase of Panchayati Raj should be properly taken into account while working out programmes of training and the required infrastructure. What is needed is systematic training at different levels, in different aspects with the purpose of enhancing the capabilities of the Panchayati Raj elected representatives along with awareness of their exacting responsibilities towards their area and people.

Prof. Tiwari's study is a comprehensive analysis of the need for training of Panchayati Raj representatives. He has marshaled arguments to bear on the problem of political education and training of the elected representatives, drawing from history, political thought, education, anthropology, economics, sociology, etc. it is in the true sense of the term an inter-disciplinary study. He has provided a framework which shows that it is possible to conduct training on a continuous basis by making apt use of the existing educational system of the country and introducing new methods and approaches focused on the specific requirements of the Panchayati Raj systems and those who are entrusted with its successful implementation. His suggestions are highly innovative.

I feel that at a time when the Union Government and various state governments are spending large sums of money in development oriented programmes for the benefit of the masses, it is necessary for the government to make training of Panchayati Raj representatives compulsory and meaningful. This will go a large way in strengthening the participation of the elected representative, particularly the marginalized sections, in the decision-making process.

There is now over a decade of experience of the working of these institutions since the passing of the 73rd Constitutional Amendment Act. Most of the state governments made only legislative changes to meet the requirements of the Amendment. Probably the spirit of the Amendment could not be fully appreciated while working out the fresh legislation. A decade of working of the Panchayati Raj institutions in the light of the Constitutional Amendment has yielded a good deal of experience and information all over the country. I am of the opinion that a new Commission or Committee must be appointed to make a total assessment of the overall progress made and make a comprehensive assessment for future revitalization. Training system should form one of the major planks in the agenda for such a Commission, when appointed. I do feel that, in the meanwhile, this single step towards accelerated, meaningful and improved training will help to make the local representative bodies vibrant, strong and effective.

I congratulate Dr. R.K. Tiwari for his painstaking effort and commend it to scholars and opinion-makers in the country.

December, 2007

T.N. Chaturvedi
Former Governor of Karnataka
and Chairman, Indian Institute of Public Administration

Preface

In the post-Independence period, the emergence of Panchayati Raj has been viewed with a feeling that the involvement of the community is an important factor in the planning and implementation of developmental activities. In this context the training of elected representatives is of great significance. Training has become all the more significant with the reservation of seats for Scheduled Castes (SCs), Scheduled Tribes (STs), and women. Besides, the weaker sections, by and large, are not only illiterate but also poor. In the case of SCs and STs, the caste factor largely also contributes in making their role marginalized to a large extent. For women, there is an additional problem of custom and tradition and which in a very significant manner militates with the kind of role and responsibility which they have to perform. The training of elected representatives has also to be seen in the context that, since the Sixth Five Year Plan, a number of programmes have been initiated for the upliftment of the poor and the weaker sections. In the absence of awareness, knowledge and understanding of these programmes as well as the procedures and processes involved in the panchayat system, the elected representatives from the weaker sections have not been able to perform and make an impact in the deliberations at all the levels of Panchayati Raj. The major problem has been illiteracy as well as lack of political education. The adult education programme too has not been very successful. What we need in the context of Panchayati Raj is the training of the elected representatives which includes: awareness about developmental programmes, some understanding about accounts, budgeting, procedures, dealing with officials, right attitude and skills, etc. For this purpose, it is necessary that a capacity building programme to be taken up with all seriousness at all levels in a continuous manner.

My interest in the capacity building and training for elected representatives of Panchayati Raj started when the Indian Institute of Public Administration (IIPA) was made one of the nodal institutions by the Ministry of Rural Development, Government of India, along with National Institute of Rural Development, Hyderabad and National Academy of Administration, Mussoorrie for conducting training of trainers programme during 1994-95. I am thankful to the then Director of the IIPA, Manik Wadhwani for assigning me the task of coordinating these training programmes along with Prof. S.N. Mishra of the Institute. With Prof. S.N. Mishra, I had discussions on many issues concerning Panchayati Raj and the development process. These discussions helped me in a better understanding of the Panchayati Raj system.

I also take this opportunity to thank Prof. Kamta Prasad, former Professor of Economics, IIPA, whose knowledge of the poor and developmental process helped me for better appreciation of the importance of capability building in the overall context of poverty alleviation.

I am thankful to Sushma Singh, the then Joint Secretary, Ministry of Rural Development, Government of India, and at present Secretary, Department for the Development of the North-Eastern Region, Government of India, for interacting on a large number of problems of training of the Pachayati Raj elected representatives. Her knowledge and understanding of the problems associated primarily with the tribals and women helped me in the formulation of a national perspective on these issues. My thanks also to A.K. Dubey, former Director, Ministry of Rural Development, Government of India, and presently Registrar, Delhi University, for his valuable suggestions on the need for awareness and training and how this has made the Kerala Panchayati Raj system, vibrant and successful.

Many thanks to Professor Aasha Kapur Mehta and Professor Sujata Singh of the IIPA with whom I interact frequently on wide ranging issues related to poverty reduction and equity. Their knowledge and understanding of the poor, provided me better insights into the role of capacity building. I am also thankful to Prof. S.N. Singh, Department of Public Administration, Lucknow University, for helpful suggestions on some chapters of the manuscript.

I am thankful to my wife Neera and my children Abhishek, Anjali and Anushree for providing me support in this work. My thanks to Ajay Singh Verma and Sonia Bajaj for providing excellent secretarial support.

December, 2007 **R.K.Tiwari**

Contents

List of Tables

1

Introduction

With the enactment of the Constitution (Seventy-third) Amendment Act, 1992, Constitutional status has been provided to the Panchayati Raj Institutions (PRIs). There are approximately three million elected representatives in the PRIs. This is the largest base of elected representatives at the local level in the world. The main features of the Constitution (Seventy-third) Amendment Act are: establishment of a three-tier structure. (Village Panchayat, Intermediate Panchayat and District Panchayat) in States which have a population of 20 lakhs and above; regular elections to Panchayats every five years; reservation of seats and offices of Chairpersons to Scheduled Castes and Scheduled Tribes in proportion to their population; reservation of not less than $1/3^{rd}$ seats and offices of Chairpersons for Women; constitution of State Finance Commissions to recommend measures to improve the finances of Panchayats; constitution of State Election Commissions; and Gram Sabhas at the village level.

As such, the Constitution (Seventy-third) Amendment Act, 1992 has brought about far reaching changes in the PRIs as units of local government. The three tier-system of panchayats is not to be regarded merely as a method of decentralisation, with a view that these institutions serve, as local agents of the state government. On the contrary, these should be regarded as the creation of democratic institutions of the people, chosen by them and answerable to them, so that the government at the local level can plan and implement schemes for economic development and ensure social justice.

In the functioning of PRIs, one important factor relates to the ignorance of the large number of members both as citizens as well as elected representatives. This problem is bound up with the heavy backlog of illiteracy in the voters as well as in the persons holding positions in the PRIs. It has been rightly pointed out that, to a large extent, illiteracy has given rise to internal problem of panchayati raj. As a consequence, some of the important problems are:

- "Problems at citizens level. Apathy, ignorance, distorted understanding and irresponsibility;
- Problems of leadership. Lack of maturity and experience, inadequate progress, gaps between the leaders and the led, irresponsibility and instability;
- Problems of inter-group adjustment. Factions, partisanship, strains between officials and non-officials, strains between Panchayats, Samitis and Parishads, strains between co-operative and Panchayat leadership, unsatisfactory central-local relations."[1]

However, to make the democratic decentralisation a success, it is imperative that the elected panchayati raj representatives should be made conscious of their responsibilities. Theoretically, the bulk of the responsibility of giving operational shape with respect to the preparation of plans for economic development and social justice in a number of important areas like: agriculture, land improvement, minor irrigation, social forestry, poverty alleviation programmes for the welfare of weaker sections, etc., has been assigned to the elected representatives of the PRIs. These new tasks, call for awareness, development of skills, understanding of administrative procedures, knowledge of financial rules and regulations and right attitudes in the elected representatives. The variety and complexity of the tasks and processes of development, have thrown up challenges for the elected representatives, which can be met to a large extent, by well organised training and orientation programmes. In this context, it is important to point out that, over the years, in a number of developmental programmes, the following problems have been noticed:

- Token implementation with emphasis on statistical achievements without bothering for substantive results, thereby affecting the credibility of government;
- Lack of proper orientation in the bureaucracy at the district and sub-district levels and its indifference towards the rural poor;
- Bureaucracy at the lower levels is not capable and also lacks the capacity to supervise and ensure proper coordination in the functioning of development programmes.

Besides, the need for training of elected representatives is all the more important due to the following factors:

- To sensitise the elected representatives about their role and responsibilities;
- Growth of technical bureaucracy at the district level and below and increasing differentiation of function within this bureaucracy, giving a new dimension to the problem of official and non-official relationship;
- The need for knowledge and skill so as to deal effectively with the complex problems of planning and implementation of developmental programmes;
- The importance of responsiveness to the people's aspirations and winning the support and cooperation of the people in the implementation processes and a spirit of service in dealing with the people.

From an integrated perspective as well as looking into the tasks and responsibilities, training of PRIs elected representa-tives may be defined as the process by which rural leadership talent is developed and energised to meet the present and future needs of the participatory system of development. It encompasses a continuing process of learning so as to induce effective performance of self-governing institutions.

Many central and state level committees which have reviewed the functioning of PRIs, by and large, expressed that the working of these institutions generally suffers due to the fact that a large number of its members are illiterate. However, almost of all these committees opined that they did not consider it necessary to lay down any educational qualifications for the elected representatives. A number of committees, both at the state and central levels strongly advocated that training is the best measure for making panchayati raj successful.[2]

In this connection, Asoka Mehta Committee (1978) pleaded that the elected representatives should treat PRIs not as power centres but as public service organisations and change-agents for social and economic development of the people. The elected representatives should have knowledge about the procedures and systems. The Universities/colleges should be associated with the training programmes for the functionaries.[3] L.M. Singhvi Committee strongly stressed the need for training and public education to strengthen the PRIs and the capabilities of voters, and elected representatives. The Committee advocated that this would be the most productive investment in democratic institution building.[4] Rajni Kothari rightly pointed out that without training, the "talk of governance would be mere sloganising."[5] He pleaded for the training of elected representatives in the art of governance through social awareness, right kind of training modules and training methodology and proper follow-up measures.

Of late, there has been a great deal of emphasis on capacity building measures for enhancing the ability of people and organisation to do what is required of them. Honadle has defined the characteristics of 'capacity' by the ability to "anticipate and influence change; make informed, intelligent decisions about policy; develop programmes to implement policy; attract and absorb resources; manage resources; and evaluate current activities to guide future action".[6] The emphasis in capacity building approach is to transfer the relevant skills and insights to the elected representatives, so as to enhance their ability to make sound decisions. It is necessary to devise suitable capacity building programmes, keeping in mind the specific needs and requirements of the elected representatives of panchayats. It has also to be seen in the context of the fact that a large number of factors must be kept in mind while designing the capacity building measures like socio-economic background, literacy level and powers and functions of PRIs at all levels. It is necessary to emphasise that training needs of the PRI representatives will vary across the states and possibly across regions within a state. However, there are certain conceptual issues which are common to all the PRIs, which "need to be internalised by all the PRIs of the country."[7] These are: "Conceptualising panchayats as institutions of self-government in the areas, and not as arms of the state government to implement some of its schemes; envisaging preparation of plans for 'economic development and social justice' in respect of the local area and implementing them as the primary tasks; recognising the right of the village community to participate in the decision-making process of the Gram Sabha; establishing the need for vertical linkages between different tiers of PRI, as each tier forms part of the edifice of Panchayati Raj."[8]

Besides the training and sensitisation of elected panchayati raj representatives, it has also come to the notice that the awareness level of voters is very low. It has also been pointed out that the Gram Sabha is virtually dysfunctional and there is no meaningful participation in the Sabha. There is a need to initiate training programmes of Gram Sabha members "to break the culture of silence."[9]

In this study, keeping the training requirement of various categories in mind, the following aspects were looked into:

- The issues concerning local government, democracy and political education in the Indian context.
- Training of elected panchayati raj representatives: 1959-69, 1970-1992 and 1993-2006.
- The implications of the Constitution (Seventy-Third) Amendment Act specifically in relation to the tasks and responsibilities at various levels.
- Assessment of training needs at various levels.
- Training programmes for different levels, i.e. District Panchayat, Intermediate Panchayat, Village Panchayat, Gram Sabha and District Planning Committee; training objectives and duration.
- Training of Panchayati Raj Representatives Organisation and Management Perspectives: role of

nodal organisation at district and sub-district levels in conducting training programmes; role of the Union Ministry of Panchayati Raj and state level departments of rural development and panchayati raj in policy formulation, monitoring and evaluation of training programmes; financial aspects of the training; resource persons; and training of trainers.

- Training of Panchayati Raj Elected Representatives: A Policy Perspective.

Training is the process by which elected representatives can gain greater effectiveness in the performance of their immediate tasks and develop potential for the discharge of responsibilities by acquiring necessary knowledge, skills and inculcating proper attitudes. Training involves learning of various kinds and in various situations. The essential components of systematically developing training programmes are:

- Identification and analysis of training needs
- Determination of training objectives
- Elements of training programme.

Analysis of responsibilities is the most important method in the determination of a systematic training programme. The steps required in this method are: a detailed study of the responsibilities, duties and tasks; and an analysis of the knowledge and skills required. The aim of this analysis is to get an overall picture of the demands of the responsibilities and the problems faced in the course of work. This analysis should provide information on: the overall purpose of the responsibilities; knowledge and skills required; and the problems faced by elected representatives in planning and implementing the programmes. For the purpose of the study, a questionnaire was prepared on the following aspects: the status of panchayat raj training, the awareness of the elected panchayati raj representatives (at all levels) about their roles and responsibilities; and to assess the training needs in a scientific manner so as to develop training programmes.

This book is divided into five chapters. Chapter one gives an overview of the need for training of elected panchayati raj representatives in the context of Constitution (Seventy-Third) Amendment Act. It also briefly discusses the problems in the context of rural development programmes, need for training, views of various committees on panchayati raj training and the conditions for the success of training programme, etc. This chapter also examines the concept of capacity building. Besides collecting material from the secondary sources, an attempt has also been made to look into the problem of training of panchayati raj representatives in Indore district (Madhya Pradesh). The purpose was to identify the awareness of the panchayati raj representatives as well as to examine the training needs in a scientific manner.

Chapter two highlights the issues concerning local government, democracy and political education. It deals with an overview of the philosophic source of local representative bodies and the contribution of John Stuart Mill with reference to the composition, functions and the role, etc., of these institutions. It has also given an overview of his thinking on the education of the poor with an emphasis on the role of local representative bodies in the political education of the poor. This chapter discusses in a comprehensive manner the experience of local government in the Indian context. It is based on the various reports which have gone into the question of the status of panchayat raj. These institutions have not been able to help the poor and the marginalised sections of the society. One critical problem has been lack of education. This apathy and lack of understanding is a product of the fact that our educational system is still based on the principles which were prevalent during the British period of Indian history. Adult education has been neglected since independence, except during the period of freedom struggle, when Mahatma Gandhi played a critical role and people participated in the freedom struggle and there was some kind of political education. Efforts made since independence have not been able to provide adult education on a sustained basis. There have been many failures due to policy ad-hocism, lack of financial support, the attitudinal problem in bureaucracy and the lack of credibility of voluntary organisations. This chapter also discusses the concept of political literacy and political education.

Chapter three deals with the training of panchayati raj representatives in three phases: 1959 to 1969, 1970 to 1992 and 1993 to 2006. This chapter examines in detail the objectives of the training programmes, organizational set-up at the central level, and state level training programmes, the course content, institutional aspect of panchayati raj training centres, training of trainers, management of training programmes, etc. This also provides an appraisal of panchayati raj training programmes in terms of: selection of institutions for training, survey of training needs, syllabus, trainers, duration, absenteeism, etc. This chapter also analyses the status of training of panchayati raj representatives as well as developments in training since 1993. This has been discussed in terms of the major workshops organised since 1993 as well as the support given by the Government of India, Ministry of Rural Development, and since May 2004, Ministry of Panchayati Raj to the state governments for the training programmes. This chapter also discusses the training of Panchayati Raj elected representatives in West Bengal and Madhya Pradesh during 1993–2001.

Chapter four discusses the training needs of elected reperesentatives at all the three levels. It surveys the magnitude of the requirements at various levels i.e. district panchayat, intermediate panchayat and village panchayat. It also provides the number of participants to be trained at all the levels state-wise. It analyses the training needs in the context of Seventh-third Amendment, taking a broad view of their functions. It also discusses the responsibilities of district planning committee and the role of subject committees in the panchayati raj system. The methodology adopted for the purpose of identification of training needs of panchayat raj representatives is based on the analysis of core characteristics of functions and tasks in each category i.e. district panchayat, intermediate panchayat and village panchayat. On this basis, training objectives, both in terms of essential requirements and desirable requirements, have been analysed. On this analysis are based the training programmes for all the three levels district, intermediate and village, Gram Sabha as well as District Planning Committee.

Chapter five deals with an organisation and management perspective in terms of institutional set-up; training programmes for various levels of panchayati raj elected representatives; need to decentralise the management of these programmes; to train the trainers with the help of higher education system; need for training committee at the district and intermediate level; and funding.

Chapter six deals with the major findings of the study as well as provide a policy framework on the training of Panchayati Raj Elected Representatives.

REFERENCES

1. Jain, Sugan Chand. 1967. *Community Development and Panchyati Raj in India.* Bombay: Allied. p. 619.
2. Study Team on Panchayati Raj (Rajasthan, 1964), Evaluation Committee on Panchayati Raj (Maharashtra, 1971), High Power Committee on Panchayati Raj (Andhra Pradesh, 1972). High Level Committee on Panchayati Raj (Gujarat, 1973), Report of the Working Group on Decentralised Planning and Panchayati Raj (Tamil Nadu, 2001). Similarly, at the central level: Committee on Block-level Planning, (1978), Committee on Panchayati Raj Institutions (1978), Working Group on District Planning (1984), Committee to Review the Existing Administrative Arrangements for Rural Development and Poverty Alleviation Programmes (1985), Committee for the Concept Paper on Panchayati Raj Institutions (1986), and Training for District Planning (1989).
3. India. Ministry of Agriculture And Irrigation. Department of Rural Development.1978. *Report of The Committee on Panchayati Raj Institutions.* New Delhi. (Chairman: Asoka Mehta). p.137.
4. India. Ministry of Agriculture. Department of Rural Development. 1986. *A Draft Concept Paper on Revitalisation of Panchayati Raj Institutions For Democracy and Development,* by Committee For the Concept Paper on Panchayati Raj Institutions. New Delhi. (Chairman: L. M. Singhvi). p. 23.
5. Kothari, Rajni. 1996. Issues in Decentralised Governance, in *Decentralised Governance in Asian Countries,* edited by Abdul Aziz and David D. Arnold. New Delhi: Sage. p. 39.
6. Honadle, Beth Walter. 1981. A Capacity-Building Framework: A Search For Concept and Purpose. *Public Administration Review,* September-October. p. 577. See also Yugandhar, B.N. 1998. Capacity Development in Public Administration in India. Dynamic Administration. Quarterly Newsletter, 42nd and 43rd

Issues, April-June, July-September. UP Regional Branch, Indian Institute of Public Administration, Lucknow. pp. 3-9.

7. National Institute of Rural Development. 2002. *Theme Papers,* All India Panchayat Adhyakshas' Sammelan, April 5-6. Hyderabad. p. 27. (Mimeo).
8. Ibid. p. 28.
9. Yatindra Singh. 2002. Decentralised Governance in Madhya Pradesh: Experiences of the Gram Sabha in Scheduled Areas. *Economic and Political Weekly,* 37(40), 5 October. p.4103.

2

Local Representative Institutions, Democracy and Political Education

The objective of this chapter is to provide a brief survey of the contribution made by John Stuart Mill with regard to the local institutions and their role in a democracy. Besides, an attempt has also been made to give Mill's views on the need of political education of the 'labouring classes' in the context of local representative institutions. An attempt has also been made to provide a brief historical overview of local self-government in India since 1882. Emphasis has been given on the working of panchayats, the lack of participation by the poor and the factors responsible for it. A brief overview has also been provided of the adult education programmes, both during pre and post-independence periods along with the need for political education of the elected representatives for the success of PRIs.

J.S. Mill on Local Representative Institutions

The philosophic source, for the strengthening of local institutions has been one of the most formidable contributions of John Stuart Mill (1806-1873). He gave a prominent place to local institutions in the context of representative government. Probably no other political thinker provided such deeper insight and attached so much importance to local representative institutions. Historically speaking, the period of Mill's writing, synchronised well, with the changes in the functioning of the Parliamentary system of government in England. Lord Ripon's resolution on the local institutions in India, in May 1882, was also deeply influenced by events in England during that period. It was also fashioned, at least in some broader aspects, on Mill's views on local institutions.

It is proposed to provide an overview of Mill's thinking on local representative institutions in the context of democracy. Mill's essay "Of Local Representative Bodies"[1] (1861) provides an analysis on various issues connected with local representative institutions. Mill was of the view that there are functions to be shared between central and local authorities on the basis of the 'principle of division of labour'. To perform these functions, separate executive officers are required. There is a need for 'popular control over those officers' through separate representative institutions both at the central and local levels. These functions should not be performed directly by the people, "Administration by the assembled people is a relic of barbarism, opposed to the whole spirit of modern life"....[2] He also analysed at length the question how the local representative bodies should be constituted and the functions that were to be assigned to these bodies. While dealing with these aspects, he was of the opinion that 'nourishment of public spirit and the development of intelligence' should be the primary focus in the constitution and the functions of the local representative bodies. He was in favour of providing a democratic basis to these institutions and vesting these institutions with powers of imposition of local taxation. The functions assigned to these bodies should consist of purely local business, "Paving, lighting, water supply, drainage, port and market regulations"..., "Police or goals and the administration of justice", etc... "administration of the poor laws, sanitary regulation, and others, which, while really interesting to the whole country, cannot consistently with the very purposes of local administration, be managed otherwise than by the localities".[3] There should be one elective body to control the business of the locality. The role of the local representative bodies should be to oversee the interest of the 'locality as a whole'. He placed a lot of emphasis, in the appointment of executive staff, for carrying out the responsibilities in local institutions, because 'Such bodies have a perpetual tendency to become joint- stock associations for carrying into effect the private jobs of their various members'.[4]

Another question, which Mill was concerned, relate to the authority and the degree of interference on the part of the central government in the matters of local affairs. He was of the view that the role of the central authority is to give instructions and that of the local authority to implement these. He pointed out the need for a constant communication by the central authority with the localities by providing information, experience, advice and overseeing enforcement of laws.

Political Education of the Labouring Classes

J.S. Mill's views on political education of the poor in the context of democracy and local government are as relevant today as they were during his times. Mill's essay *The Claims of Labour*[5] (1845) constitute his thinking on the subject of poverty and the need for educating the poor in the context of representative government. Mill had a special concern for "the labouring classes', who during his time were removed from the "power privilege, and the standard of living". In fact, his "Chapter on Socialism" (1870) condemned poverty as the 'first among existing social evils' and went to the extent of stating that the condition of 'the labouring classes' in European countries "is more wretched then that of most tribes of savages who are known to us."[6] Mill categorically stated that it is basically a failure of the 'social arrangements' and criticised the fact that the wages of labour are totally insufficient to provide the "physical and moral necessities of the population in any tolerable measure"[7]. Besides, poverty and long hours of work left the labouring classes little time for other aspects of life. This class was devoid of "dignity, self-respect and independence" as well as little chance for their economic improvement. Mill's views on poverty and the conditions which governed the life of the wage earning classes in England during those times have been studied also empirically. A major study on 'Poverty'[8] by Rowntree, conducted in the city of York, England (1899), confirmed by and large Mill's views expressed nearly forty years earlier (1859). As a matter of fact, this study further pointed out that nearly 30 per cent of the population was living in poverty. The wages paid for unskilled labours were 'insufficient to provide food, shelter, and clothing adequate to maintain a family of moderate size in a state of bare physical efficiency'[9]. Rowntree also mentioned a similar study conducted between (1887-1892) in London district by Charles Booth. This study, titled *Life and Labour of the People in London* (17 volumes), estimated that 30.7 per cent of the total population of London were living in poverty.[10]

In the essay, "*Local Representative Bodies*" (1861), Mill viewed local institutions as the chief instruments of public education of the citizens. He was convinced that local institutions provide an opportunity to the mass of the population to participate in the "conduct of the general affairs of the community'. The local institutions also provide to the elected functionaries in local executive positions and "to act, for public interests, as well as to think and to speak, and the thinking cannot all be done by proxy".[11]

In the essay, "The Claims of Labour" (1845), Mill was of the view that illiteracy, ignorance and lack of awareness, in a way debarred 'the labouring classes' from effective political participation. In the context of democracy, he was concerned 'by the low state of their understandings.'[12] He further highlighted this fact by stating "their incapacity to observe what is before their eyes; their inability to comprehend or believe purposes in others which they have not been taught to expect, and are not conscious of in themselves – are the known characteristics of persons of low intellectual faculties...."[13] As a result, Mill was of the opinion that these people have "deficiency in the power of reasoning and calculation, which makes them insensible to their own direct personal interests."[14] Mill was concerned with the question how to "instil into these people the commonest worldly wisdom", so as to "improve their conduct in every relation of life, and clear the soil for the growth of right feelings and worthy propensities."[15] He exhorted the higher and middle classes "to submit to a very considerable sacrifice of their own means, for improving the condition of the poor. "[16] He was of the view that for this condition of the poor, the higher classes are responsible as they had not 'fulfilled their duties as governors.'[17] The illiteracy of the poor, is a consequence of the non-fulfillment of the duties of the higher classes, which had resulted in allowing the labouring classes 'to grow up so ignorant and uncultivated as to be open to these mischievous delusions.'[18] Mill in the essay, "On the Probable Futurity of the Labour Classes" (1849), was of the opinion that the future of the labouring classes depends "on the degree in which they can be made rational beings."[19] He was convinced that "until there is a change in themselves, there can be no lasting improvement in their outward condition."[20]

Mill was deeply influenced by the thinking of the "Radical representatives"[21] of the middle class which during the 19th century saw mass education as a political necessity. This group pleaded that education was the most powerful instrument for changing men's mind and outlook and it is through education alone that the working classes could be brought within the "orbit of civilization". They believed that there is close link between education and political action. This group felt that besides educating the workers in their occupations, there is also a need to educate them and that "the ascertained truths of political science should be early taught to the labouring classes, and *correct* political information should be constantly and industriously disseminated amongst them."[22] Thereby the poor might also "be made to understand their political position in society, and the duties that belong to it – that they are in a great measure the architects of their own fortune; that what others can do for them is trifling indeed, compared with what they can do for themselves."[23]

It was Mill's considered opinion that education is the main basis for the improvement in the condition of the labouring classes.[24] Democracy is not possible without an educated electorate. Democracy requires of its citizens an active participation in the processes of government. To achieve this, he was of the view that it is the obligation of the government "to promote the education of its citizens by all possible formal and informal means, including participation and the provision of a favourable total environment."[25] He contemplated that the education for the labouring classes should not be confined to a simple literacy and numeracy.[26] He desired that as far as education of the poor is concerned, "Such a system of education should exist as will give to the mass of mankind not learning but common-sense, practical judgement in ordinary affairs, and shall enable them to see that a thing is wrong when it is wrong.'[27] The education of the citizen should comprise of some knowledge of history, constitution, workings of central and local government; training in thinking and practice in discussion and reasoned argument. He emphasised the need for education for democracy. This education, according to Mill, is not a one shot affair but an on-going process, which develops the potential of the people, as well as enlarges their "communal experience".

James Bryce has been another political thinker who had drawn the attention to the problem of democracy and the backward races.'[28] He was of the view that a society divided by language, religion or castes distinctions, normally lead to 'mutual distrust and animosity'. This, in turn, prevents the people to act together. Bryce also pointed out in a very insightful manner that "Political institutions ought to be framed with careful regard to social conditions."[29] He was of the view that greater inequality lead to exploitation of the poorer classes by the stronger and, in such a situation, "the ruling sections are likely to legislate and administer for own benefit and oppress those beneath them."[30] He was of the view that there is no use of giving democratic institutions to the people who do not know 'how to use these'? In such a situation, a representative democracy 'is sure to be perverted, because the people have no means of restraining those who will seek to turn it to their own ends.'[31] Bryce was of the opinion that to fit the people for free self-government, 'knowledge and experience as well as intelligence' are needed.

LOCAL SELF INSTITUTIONS IN INDIA: 1882-1947

It is a matter of common knowledge that local institutions in India as a part of representative organisation "responsible to a body of electors, enjoying wide powers of administration and taxation, and functioning both as a school for training in responsibility and a vital link in the chain of organisms that make up the Government of the country, is a British creation."[32] The rural local bodies in India developed, in a very slow manner, unlike the urban local bodies, which started much earlier. The first rural local institutions introduced in 1869 were quasi-official committees. In 1882, a definite policy of establishing a network of rural local authorities was enunciated. It is also true that these institutions did not develop out of ancient village communities which were based on necessary privilege or caste and with limited duties i.e. revenue collection and protection of life and property. As such, there is difference between earlier panchayats and the local institutions established by the British.

Ripon's Resolution

Prior to Lord Ripon's Local Self Government Resolution, 1882, a number of attempts were made for building up representative councils from the village to provincial level. Mayo's Resolution of 14th December 1870 emphasised that for the successful management of funds devolved to education, sanitation, medical and local public works, local supervision was necessary. Mayo's approach was to train Indians in public administration "We must gradually associate with ourselves in the Government of this country more of the native element. We have neglected this too much. Were we to quit India tomorrow, we should leave whole Provinces in which would not be found a man capable of administrating [*sic*] the affairs of a small district. It can only be a work of time;..., so in India do I believe that we shall find the best assistance from natives in our administration, not by competitive examination or the sudden elevation of ill educated and incapable men, but by quietly entrusting as many as we can with local responsibility, and instructing them in the management of their own district affairs."[33] In 1873, Charles Trevelyan submitted to a Parliamentary Committee the need for building up such representative councils in India. He observed that these institutions "would be schools of self-government for the whole of India, the largest step yet taken towards teaching its 200,000,000 of people to govern themselves... ."[34] Besides, the Famine Commission in 1880 also recommended the extension of local self-government, as a means of facilitating the relief of local distress.

Lord Ripon was convinced that the new local-government machinery should not be established only to suit administrative requirements but political education and administrative efficiency should be put into perspective. The Resolution also emphasised the education of the popularly elected members of rural and urban local bodies as well as of the electorate "It is not, primarily, with a view to improvement in administration that this measure is put forward and supported. It is chiefly desirable as an instrument of political and popular education."[35] It is interesting to point out that, by political and popular education Ripon meant "the acquisition of skill and experience necessary for the management of their local affairs. Its nature was political because it involved the education of a political body, a popular representative agency of self-government."[36] The Ripon Resolution proposed setting of municipal bodies and boards at the district level consisting of a large majority of elected non-officials as well as rural local boards, with two-thirds of whose membership was composed of elected representatives. Ripon anticipated "a serious political danger arising from a rigid bureaucracy and a rising Indian middle class, both pulling in two opposite directions."[37] Ripon was critical of the bureaucracy because Lord Mayo's Resolution of 1870 dealing with local self-government was almost set to naught due to the indifference of the bureaucracy. Ripon was aware of the fact that there was lack of political perspective in the district officers. It was for this reason that Ripon was emphatic for the revival of local bodies and making them popular, strong, autonomous and broad based. Ripon pointed out this in the following words: "India is governed by a bureaucracy, which, though I sincerely believe it to be the best bureaucracy that the world has ever seen, has still the faults and the dangers which belong to every institution of that kind;

among those faults is conspicuously a jealousy of allowing non-officials to interfere in any way whatever with any portion, however restricted, of the administration of the country."[38] On the other hand, Ripon's proposal also served to placate the claims of the new Indian middle class so as to "provide a legitimate outlet for the ambitions and aspirations."[39] It was in this context that Ripon believed that an extension of the elective system and reduction of official control "will not only have an immediate effect in promoting gradually and safely the political education of the people", but "will also pave the way for further advances in the same direction as that education becomes fuller and more widespread."[40] It was Rippon's conviction that this resolution though would provide the government officers the power to check acts of local bodies but not dictate them "If we really mean to train the natives of this country to take a substantial part in the administration of local affairs, we must give them fair opportunities of doing so, and must be content to see them make mistakes that they may learn by experience, which is the best of all teachers in the practical business of life, the mischievous consequences of unsound principles, or slothful neglect of duty."[41]

However, the development of local self-government, as proposed in the Ripon resolution, was halting due to a number of factors. In fact, local boards were not constituted in large parts of British India. The Royal Commission upon Decentralisation in India (1907-09) in its report pointed out a number of problems which hindered the growth of local self-government in India: failure to develop the principle of election, appointment of official presidents as well as the fact that the boards practically became the department of government administration, etc. It was further pointed out that "in the present circumstances, they can never become, as Lord Ripon intended them to be, effective instruments of local self-government."[42] In connection with the political education of the people, the Report pointed out "The political education of any people must necessarily be slow, and local self-government of the British type could not at once take root in Indian soil."[43]

Gokhale's Contribution

It is important to mention the role played by Gopal Krishan Gokhale in the development of local representative institutions in India. Gokhale's views on local government are reflected in his 'Note on Decentralisation', submitted to the Royal Commission on Decentralisation (1907-09). He was an ardent champion of democratisation and bringing local institutions at the district level and below, into the democratic process. He felt, "The only remedy lies in carrying a substantial measure of decentralization down to the villages and in building up local self-government from there."[44] In a comprehensie manner, this "Note" also examines the functioning of local government from 1882 to 1906. In one of his speeches in moving a Resolution in the Imperial Legislative Council in 1912 for appointing a committee to inquire into the adequacy or otherwise of the resources at the disposal of local bodies, he pointed out, "The district administration, however, continues to be where it was 100 years ago, and local self-government too continues to be where it was carried by the late Marquis of Ripon about 30 years ago: and I strongly feel, my Lord, that there must be important reforms introduced in respect of both these, in order that all parts of the administrative machinery should be brought into closer correspondence with one another."[45] He also pointed out that the resources at the disposal of local bodies are very slender and pleaded that the resources at their disposal be largely increased.

He was of the opinion that one of the important functions of the local bodies is to develop 'civic spirit and raise the level of general intelligence among the people.'[46] He further valued the role of local self-government by emphasising the fact that "it teaches men of different castes and creeds, who have long been kept more or less apart to work together for a common purpose."[47] He was convinced that local self government is 'a training ground, a school of political education for our people.'[48] Gokhale was one of the first leaders who strongly felt the need for local initiative and responsibility at the district level and below. He was convinced that self-government and democracy ought to begin from the village and work upwards.

Education of the depressed classes was another subject very strongly advocated by Gokhale. He was aware of the fact that the treatment given to the low castes in India was humiliating and painful. For this, he blamed "the attitude of our educated men towards this class."[49] He further pointed out "I think all fair-minded persons will have to admit that it is absolutely monstrous that a class of human beings, with bodies similar to our own, with brains that can think and with hearts that can feel, should be perpetually condemned to a low life of utter wretchedness, servitude and mental and moral degradation, and that permanent barriers should be placed in their way so that it should be impossible for them ever to overcome them and improve their lot."[50] He was aware of the fact that the lack of education and ignorance of masses was a great obstacle in the development and was convinced that "Only so long as the people of India are kept in ignorance and their faculties are forced to lie dormant, that they do not raise any objection to the present system of administration. The moment education quickens those faculties and clears their vision, they range themselves against a continuance of the system."[51]

Under the Montagu-Chelmsford Reforms of 1919, local self-government became a transferred subject and was brought under the domain of Indian ministers in the provinces. To make local self-government both fully representative and responsible, the reforms had suggested that, "There should be as far as possible, complete popular control in local bodies, and the largest possible independence for them of outside control."[52] By 1925, a number of provinces passed village panchayat Acts and by 1926, some native states had also adopted village panchayat laws. Subsequently, similar laws were adopted by other states also. The Government of India Act, 1935 also gave an impetus to the evolution of the panchayats in the country.

Hugh Tinker, while concluding the gains from local government experience, termed it as "an apprentice – period of trial and error." However, he was of the view that the local government 'chief contribution was to provide training for politicians and electorate...' He cited a number of leaders who served an apprenticeship in local government: S.N. Banerjea, Pheroze Shah Mehta, G.K. Gokhale, Vallabhbhai Patel, Sarojini Naidu, Sikandar Hyat Khan and Khwaja Nazimuddin, S.G.H. Hidayutallah, K.N. Katju, Sri Prakasa, M.L. Saksena, H.S. Suhrawaddy and S.P. Tandon, etc.[53] However, in a major study on the shaping of a public culture in Surat city, covering the period between 1852-1928, Douglas Haynes observed that "these institutions gave little voice to underclass groups..." and "a tiny group of educated figures monopolised the critical symbolic skills needed to approach alien rulers."[54]

PANCHAYATI RAJ: POST INDEPENDENCE PERIOD

Constituent Assembly Debates

However, it is interesting to note that in the Constituent Assembly when the "Resolution on the Aims and Objects of free India's Constitution", was introduced on 13th December, 1946, there was no mention of the place of villages in an Independent India, their role in its government and the meaning of Swaraj to the Indian village. It is a part of India's constitutional history now that, due to the omission of villages, a large number of members were very agitated and disappointed. They were further provoked, by Dr.B.R. Ambedkar's statement as Chairman of the Scrutiny Committee. "I hold that these village republics have been the ruination of India. I am, therefore, surprised that those who condemn provincialism and communalism should come forward as champions of the village. What is the village but a sink of localism, a den of ignorance, narrow-mindedness and communalism? I am glad that the Draft Constitution has discarded the village and adopted the individual as its unit."[55]

Leaving aside the larger debate on this issue, a number of members strongly advocated the education and training of the village people, so as to generate public spirit and awareness about political and civic responsibilities. It was also mentioned that, in the absence of awareness and education, "the local influential classes will absorb to themselves all the powers and privileges that will be given by the Panchayat System and they will utilise it for their selfish motives."[56] A group of members also advocated that the purpose of democracy is not only to bring people periodically for electing Assembly and Parliament candidates, but the broader and more significant purpose through the local-self government will be to provide training ground for democracy and sharing responsibility. In the absence of this, under this Constitution there will be two classes "a new ruling class at the helm of affairs and at the bottom there will be the common man exercising a vote once in five years."[57] It was advocated by a few members that the village panchayats will be an extension of democracy to the lowest ground. It was also pointed out that the very essence of democracy is the effective participation of the individual in the actual governance of the country "it alone makes for the strength and efficiency of the Centre... democracy of conscious effective citizens is much stronger and more efficient, from any point of view than any other form of government...."[58]

During the debate on this issue the overwhelming opinion of the Constituent Assembly members was for recognising the village and giving it a place in the Indian polity. As a result, a new clause was inserted in the Constitution and adopted with no dissent. This is how the Article 40 of the Constitution 'The State shall take steps to organise village panchayats and endow them with such powers and authority as may be necessary, to ensure them to function as units of self-Government's forms part of the Directive Principles of State Policy'.

Community Development

The commencement of Community Development and National Extension Service (1952) created for the first time a development entity separate from the revenue administration. The Balvantray Mehta Committee (1957) looked into institutional framework of the community development projects. This committee categorically pointed out that there should be administrative decentralisation for the effective implementation of the development programme. The decentralised administrative system should be under the control of local bodies: "Development cannot progress without responsibility and power. Community development can be real only when the community understands its problems, realises its responsibilities, exercises the necessary powers through its chosen representatives and maintains a constant and intelligent vigilance on local administration."[59] The Committee recommended the establishment of statutory elective local bodies and devolution of the necessary resources, power and authority to them.

In this context, the Committee also dealt with the need for social education, so as to create a new outlook, new values and attitudes on the part of the people. This involves broadly teaching adults about citizenship and democracy and teaching them to read and write, Mehta was convinced that panchayat members, have to discharge their responsibilities in a progressive and democratic manner. He also suggested a broad curriculum: meaning of citizenship, democracy, elementary knowledge of history, geography and social conditions of the country, ethics, etc. He was keen to energise people's organisation for group action so as to give an impetus to the entire development programe by their active involvement as well as to build up local leadership. For this purpose, he pleaded for training and education in citizenship in the widest sense of the term. Besides, he also pleaded for the need of some instruction in elementary development planning, combined with general citizenship topics, to be taught to the panchayat members and other adults so as to provide them some understanding and grasp of developmental programmes. He also suggested to organise village leaders camps. The acceptance of the recommendations of Balvantray Mehta Study Team, in fact, initiated a new era of PRIs in October, 1959. By 1977, these institutions covered 96 per cent of the villages and 92 per cent of the rural population of the country.

Jayaprakash Narayan's Contribution

Jayaprakash Narayan was another important thinker. Panchayati Raj had an important place in his scheme of things. He wanted to move ahead of the western concept of democracy by emphasising on people's participation in government i.e. "participating democracy". He was of the view that the democracy should be like a pyramid – "narrow a the top and broad at the bottom". In the devolution of power, defence, foreign affairs, inter-state relations, currency, import and exports regulation, national unity are the tasks only of the central government and all the rest should be exercised by the lower organs. He was also critical of the fact that the initiative for panchayati raj in the early sixties came "not from the political motive of broadening the base of our democracy..., but from the anxiety to obtain full public cooperation in the execution of development programmes."[60] He also laid down certain conditions for the success of panchayati raj education of the people, control of the people without party interference and a real devolution of power and giving full opportunity to the people to shoulder responsibility. He was also of the view that we should not distrust the ability and intelligence of the common people and confidence in their abilities. As far as the role of the official element was concerned, he felt that the role of the collector should be nominal, only as a representative of the state government. He was of the view that the civil servants should be accountable to panchayati raj. The control of resources should remain in the hands of the panchayat. He placed a lot of importance on the Gram Sabha and wanted to make it a statutory collective body. He envisaged a lot of functions to this body, including the budget. He was aware of the backwardness and the ignorance of the village people, but he was convinced that "by actually handling responsibility that the necessary competence and ability for self-government can be acquired; and secondly, the remedy for backwardness is not to deny the people their sovereign rights, but to enlighten, educate and train them with as much expedition as possible."[61]

Asoka Mehta Committee Report

The Report of the Committee on Panchayati Raj Institutions (1978), categorised these institutions in three phases: (i) the phase of ascendancy (1959-64), (ii) the phase of stagnation (1965-69), and (iii) the phase of decline (1969-77). This Committee, while giving the reasons for the disillusionment with the working of the panchayats, pointed out in a strong terms that their failure was due to a number of inadequacies. The Report observed, "PRIs are dominated by economically or socially privileged sections of society and have as such facilitated the emergence of oligarchic forces yielding no benefits to weaker sections. The performance of PRIs has also been vitiated by political factionalism, rendering developmental trusts either warped or diluted. Corruption, inefficiency, scant regard for procedures, political interference in day-to-day administration, parochial loyalties, motivated actions, power concentration instead of service consciousness – all these have seriously limited the utility of panchayati raj for the average villager."[62] Besides, democratisation did not affect the traditional leadership, however, it did provide "democratic seed-drilling".

E.M.S. Namboodiripad in his "Note on the Report of the Committee on Panchayati Raj Institutions"[63] pleaded for an integrated administration from the centre down to the elected panchayat bodies to control "the permanent services at the district and lower levels." He also advocated that these bodies should help the working people in their day-to-day struggles against their "oppressors and exploiters" and to bring about better mobilisation and organisation of the mass of the working people in the rural areas. He viewed these institutions without difference between 'developmental and regulatory functions'.

Related Developments

In 1985, a Committee set up by the Ministry of Agriculture, Department of Rural Development, Government of India, "To Review the Existing Administrative Arrangements for Rural Development and Poverty Allieviation Programmes", expressed that there has been "stagnation and later a decline" in the functioning of these institutions in many parts of the country. It was suggested by this Committee that rural development programmes could become realistic and meaningful only if "people's representatives are actively involved in the local level planning, design, formulation and implementation of these schemes and in selection of beneficiaries...."[64] For this purpose, it was suggested that there is a need to revitalise and endow PRIs with necessary resources and powers to discharge the functions and responsibilities assigned to them.

The same sentiments were also voiced by the Committee for the Concept Paper on Panchayati Raj Institutions (CCPPRI) (1986). "From the very start, it was an onerous struggle for survival for the Panchayati Raj Institutions in the face of hostile and adverse encounter with institutions of established power."[65]

L.C. Jain, in a major study on rural development programmes, emphasized: "Panchayats must be given the stature of being units of self-government as envisaged in the Constitution and their elections made mandatory and entrusted to the Election Commission. Their functions should be scheduled on the lines of the Centre, State and Concurrent Lists, and their share in financial resources determined by statutory State Finance Commissions."[66]

Rajiv Gandhi's Contribution

It has been rightly pointed out that, since 1985, a search began for appropriate institutional arrangements so that the benefits reached the poor. Rajiv Gandhi, the then Prime Minister played a very important role in the revitalization of the panchayati raj institutions as well as bringing them in the mainstream of the development process "The experience of the vast majority of our people at the grassroots has been that at the interface between the people and administration, the administration is unresponsive, inefficient, unsympathetic, often callous, sometimes even cruel to those whom they are meant to serve."[67] He also participated in five workshops for the district magistrates on responsive administration. The purpose was to make district administration more efficient and effective. All these developments, culminated in the introduction of the Constitution (Sixty-fourth) Amendment Bill in the Lok Sabha on 15th May, 1989. Rajiv Gandhi, while introducing the Constitution (Sixty-fourth) Amendment Bill, 1989, pointed out that the working of the PRIs has shown that in many states they have become weak and ineffective due to a large number of factors like – failure to hold regular elections, prolonged supersessions, inadequate representation of the weaker sections, inadequate resources and inadequate power responsibilities. While introducing the Bill, the Prime Minister said, "Our Bill goes beyond merely planning for economic development. It lays upon the Panchayats the even heavier responsibility of planning for social justice. It will not do to romanticise life in our villages. Life there is hard. Life there is exacting. Life there is, in many ways, exploitative and oppressive."[68] The Constitution (Sixty-fourth) Amendment Bill was passed by the Lok Sabha on 10th August, 1989. However, it could not be enacted as it was not approved by the Rajya Sabha. In the meanwhile, Lok Sabha Elections were held in December, 1989 and, following the polls, a revised 69th Constitution Amendment Bill was introduced on 7th September, 1990 in the Lok Sabha. But this Bill was not even taken up for consideration and lapsed with the dissolution of the Lok Sabha.

Constitution (Seventy-third) Amendment

It is interesting to point out that, at the time of moving the resolution on the (Seventy-third) Amendment Bill in the Parliament, on 1st December 1992, the Minister of State for Rural Development, pointed out that these institutions are necessary to sustain democracy in the country.[69] Besides, the full potential of these institutions has not been realized in many parts of the country. The Resolution further pointed out the factors which prevented the growth and development of these institutions are: imposing nominated bodies, irregular elections, elected bodies have been superseded or suspended, etc. However, the most important factor mentioned by the Minister, relate to these bodies being dominated by economically and socially privileged sections of the rural society. These sections utilised PRIs to serve their class and vested interests. It is in this background that the Resolution pointed out the need for constitutional guarantee to certain basic features of PRIs. It was also mentioned that the reservations for Scheduled Castes and Scheduled Tribes and women would bring the members of these communities to a "position in which they would be able to participate effectively in the functioning of these bodies."[70]

Participation of the Weaker Sections

However, a number of studies conducted since 1993 in different parts of the country in the context of the participation of the weaker sections reveal the following:

- Illiteracy is higher among women and is more striking at the gram panchayat level. However, this does not hold true for the women members at the district panchayat and intermediate panchayat levels.
- Self motivation to contest elections is low among women specially at the gram panchayat level.
- Most of the women, especially at the level of gram panchayat, are first time members and ignorant about the political processes.
- At the gram panchayat level, not only the women and the members from Scheduled Castes and Scheduled Tribes are illiterate, but also a large segment belong to below the poverty line.
- The women members, due to illiteracy, are unable to fulfill their decision making roles and they are controlled mostly by their husbands.
- The women are not aware about their powers, responsibilities and authority at least at the gram panchayat level. It has been rightly pointed out that women have come in "with their social and economic disadvantages – mostly non-literate, with little productive assets, largely dependent on wage labour and into a rural society that has fixed places for various castes and gender. These cannot be changed by a wave of the constitutional amendment wand."[71]

All these factors result in a situation where their participation is seriously handicapped because participation does not exist in the abstract and in a participatory structure "overall forms of social inequality and oppression are usually reflected and maintained."[72] It has also revealed that many of the people elected, especially those in the reserved categories, are very poor. In attending the meetings of the Panchayat Raj, they often have to forgo a day's wage. The reservations for women and other categories have not led to their participation in decision-making in local bodies."[73]

Another important aspect which need to be highlighted relates to the fact that the "traditional upper caste hold is still strong." The dominant caste act as parallel decision making organisation in all matters of the villages. It has been rightly pointed out: "The panchayats today mirror the dirt in the village life and its social relations. Any change in the status quo is resisted, sometimes violently. Reservation for Scheduled Castes, Scheduled Tribes and women is accepted in form but seldom in substance. The weaker sections of society are at the receiving end."[73]

Empowerment is an expression which is frequently being used since the last few years for empowering the ordinary people and disadvantaged groups of society. Reservation does provide them a notional sense of empowerment. Andre Beteille has rightly observed, "the advocates of empowerment seek to alter...the social composition of these institutions and not necessarily their mode of functioning..."[74] He further articulated his views by observing: "The belief that they can by themselves bring about a radical or even a perceptible redistribution of power is no more than wishful thinking."[75] Besides, in democratic participation, "There are a number of intellectual resources that increase the likelihood that an individual will attempt some participatory act and that it will be successful. These include: information about politics, issues, channels of communications, and the rules of political participation and skills in manipulating these channels of access. Skills in written and oral expression, in reasoning, and in manipulating others are important."[76] However, in the Indian context, even in the pre-Independence period, it was observed that, after introduction of the elective principle in the district boards, the nominated councilors withdrew from direct participation in the municipal arena as they found themselves: "ill-equipped to deal with the sophisticated and mystifying system of municipal law, the ritualised rules of procedure at work in council meetings, and the rhetoric of political rights and responsibilities to which councillors needed to appeal in effectively pressing their cases."[77] This position has not changed at least in the matters of local government both urban and rural. It is a well known fact that the Scheduled Castes/Scheduled Tribes are still dependent on the dominant groups for the articulation of their views. However, even this articulation makes little contribution to their well being. What is needed is that the poor Scheduled Castes and Scheduled Tribes and women to generate their own intellectual equipments and languages to confront many of the dominant assumptions of the polity.

In the context of Constitution (Seventy-third) Amendment, T.V. Sathyamurthy observed that the political power will only help the rural local elites but 'will leave the poorest 40-50 per cent of the society untouched and, perhaps, even worse off (if that can be imagined!).'[78] He further pointed out "there are two societies in India, one of which is poised to receive marginal benefits from the broadening of the institutional base of power that is being promoted under two recent amendments to the Indian Constitution on the subject of decentralisation and elected self-governing local authorities. The other is left to fend for itself under regional, national and international conditions more hostile than ever before experienced, at least in India's post-colonial history."[79] The comments of Sathyamurthy are very revealing as in this article he was reviewing a report on the functioning of panchayats in West Bengal. As it is widely known, in West Bengal the panchayats have done a lot of work and even tried to bring the marginalized and weaker sections into the mainstream of the functioning of the panchayat through their various programmes and activities. Sudha Pai, on the basis of empirical study of Meerut district, observed that in the present panchayati raj system at all levels, an elite democracy functions, which does not allow the large majority to participate in decision making. As a result "panchayat institutions in U.P., faithfully reflect the unequal and segmented society in which they are embedded and are an arena of contestation rather than cooperation among various caste segments over resources and benefits."[80] "The working of the panchayats in Uttar Pradesh" by Lieten et.al. concluded that the participation of the women, Scheduled Castes and Backward Classes at all levels of local government "has remained nominal and so far has done little to enhance the participation of these groups in village affairs."[81] It has been pointed out that social dominance, low levels of literacy and cultural traditions are important factors leading to low levels of participation of this group. As a consequence, the Panchayati Raj "has not really helped to bring the fruits of development."[82]

The role of women in Panchayati Raj raises two questions – first, the question of their capacity to effectively represent the general interests of the community; and secondly, "their capacity to conceptualise and effectively represent the interests of women in the community".[83] The basic problem which the women members of panchayat suffer has been due to lack of education, articulation and self-confidence[84]. It is also due to their first exposure to a political role.

Due to the continuing hold of powerful local vested interests on village level institutions, "The mere placing of a few women in positions of authority within panchayats is unlikely to change this scenario as long as the strongman's position remains intact, and anchored to the property structure which excludes the majority from the fruits of wealth. The argument that political rights mean little without economic and other rights has by now become a classic theme in Political Science".[85] The Participatory Research in Asia team in a study of the working of the Gram Sabha in Gujarat, Haryana, Himachal Pradesh, Kerala and Uttar Pradesh, observed that there is lack of awareness on the part of the members not only about the time and the venue of the meetings, but also about the usefulness of such meetings. While talking to the members present in the meeting, the researchers felt that many of them were confused about the role of the Gram Gabha. Some of them perceived Gram Sabha meetings as political meetings and that the only function of Gram Sabha was to prepare the list of beneficiaries under different anti-poverty programmes."[86] The study further pointed out "The scholars observe that most of the heads of the panchayats lack skills in conducting meetings in a manner that could promote wider participation and discussion of the issues affecting the village. Issues of social justice and internal dynamics of the village have rarely been agenda items in the Gram Sabha meetings."[87] As such, in the Indian context particularly with reference to Scheduled Castes, Scheduled Tribes, women and other backward classes, especially at the village level fail to participate in the political process as they are uneducated and do not have the capacity and motivation. The studies referred to in the preceding pages have shown that, by and large, "lower–status groups and the psychologically handicapped are prone to feel bewildered and helpless; they are, in general, more susceptible to feelings of alienation, anomie, and pessimism–both personal and political."[88] Political participation is not "natural", but must be learnt, and for learning to occur, one must have capacity, motivation, and opportunity."[89]

Adult Education

The analysis given in the preceding section clearly underscores that the Scheduled Castes and Scheduled Tribes and women have not been able to participate effectively in the functioning of these institutions. An important factor has been illiteracy. The total number of illiterate population in the country as given in the (Census of India 2001: Provisional Population Tables) estimated that the total number of illiterates in the country is to the tune of 29,62,08,952. It also provides that the crude literacy rate in 2001 in category of males is 64.13 and in case of females is 45.84. The literacy rate has registered a significant increase from 16.67 per cent in 1951 to 55.30 per cent in 2001. However, due to rapid increase in population, the absolute number of non-literates is more now than at the time of Independence.

For this purpose, it is necessary to provide some kind of an overview of the educational system in the country from the perspective of how during the British period of Indian history, no policy measures were taken for rectifying the problem of adult illiteracy. The whole emphasis of the British was to educate a class of persons who could act as the interpretors between the rulers and the ruled. As a consequence, the system of education was meant for the ruling classes, who realised it to modernise themselves and to strengthen and perpetuate their own positions. It hardly reached the masses. Some changes were made in the post-independence period but as has been pointed out "But to the extent education did reach the masses, it mainly domesticated them to accept the existing social order... Essentially, it was a system that helped domination and domestication rather than liberation."[90] "The poor people still remained outside the system: vast numbers of their children did not go to school; a large proportion of those enrolled dropped out very early; and the percentage of literacy"[91] was not very significant.

Prior to 1917, the problem of liquidation of adult illiteracy did not receive any attention. However, issue of adult illiteracy received some attention after the Government of India Act, 1919 was passed. In a large number of provinces like Punjab, Central Provinces, Bombay and Madras, night schools were established for educating the adult illiterates. These schools were established by different organisations like cooperative societies, local bodies, semi-official and non-official agencies, etc. Besides the curriculum included grounding in the three R's and elementary knowledge of cooperative accountancy. In fact, between 1921 and 1937, there were 11,158 institutions mostly in Provinces like Madras, Punjab, Bengal, Bombay with enrolment of 2,90,000 peoples.

The most important contribution in the field of adult education was made between 1937 to 1947 when the Congress Ministries were formed in a number of provinces. Syed Mahmud, the Education Minister of Bihar, in his capacity as the Chairman of the Adult Education Committee in 1939, provided the philosophy governing adult education. "Adult Education as a foundation on which must be based the development of the social, economic and political life of this ancient land of ours. As long as the masses remain steeped in illiteracy and ignorance, economic and social upbuilding of the nation will remain a pious dream...." "An illiterate man is outside of politics, and before he can be brought in, he must first be taught the alphabet. Without this, there can be no politics – only rumours, gossip, tales, superstitions."[92] It is very interesting to point out that Syed Mahmud was aware of the radical movement of Britain which has been described in the previous section and he emphasised to re-orient this adult education in the Indian context with emphasis on : (i) to teach the illiterate adult about the three R's and (ii) to impart knowledge closely related to his working life as well as to give him a grounding in citizenship. Syed Mahmud, during the period of 1937-1947, also made a very interesting innovation by organising literacy campaigns as a purely voluntary movement and entrusting the task to the teachers and students of the Province to devote their summer vacation only to the liquidation of illiteracy. For this purpose, primary, middle schools were required to conduct adult literacy classes and were paid a grant-in-aid of annas 5 per adult made literate; some private associations also conducted literacy classes. Similarly, colleges and high schools were also required to organise these classes. Large scale employers of labours also organised. However, no grant-in-aid was paid to them. During 1938, around 4,50,000 adult were made literate. It is also interesting to point out that this campaign was conducted by a Provincial Mass Literacy Committee appointed by the Government. Similarly, District Committees and Sub-Divisional Committees were also created for this purpose. As a result during 1939, around 4,13,482 became literate and the number of literacy workers was 20,567, out of which 5,267 were primary school teachers. There were 18,878 literacy centres. This literacy campaign was really organised on a large scale and it has been described "the most impressive Government campaign conducted in India in modern times. Similar campaigns were organised in the provinces of Bombay, Mysore, etc. In Bombay, the emphasis was on training in good citizenship, rather than merely instruction in three R's".

With the onset of the Second World War, this movement almost declined. Although since Independence, efforts are being made in this direction "but never recaptured the spirit of those early days.[93] With Independence, came the idea of radically changing the entire educational system in the country. However, nothing much has come out in this direction. As far as the adult literacy is concerned, J.P. Naik opined in the following words. "The liquidation of adult illiteracy is the most important programme of national development and on it depends several other programmes such as agricultural production, family planning, etc. This sector has been criminally neglected and it is extremely desirable to undertake a large-scale programme in this sector and to liquidate mass illiteracy in a few years – five or ten at the most".[94]

Discussing about the illiteracy, the Education Commission, in 1967, opined, "The circumstances of modern life condemn the illiterate to live an inferior existence. He has little prospect of a reasonable income. He remains isolated from sophisticated social processes, such as democratic government and commercial marketing. The uneducated is not in reality a free citizen. Illiteracy as a mass phenomenon blocks economic and social progress, affects economic productivity, population control, national integration and security and improvement in health and sanitation."[95] However, it is significant to note that after independence, many literacy drives were organised on state and local basis, but these efforts were not much successful and the Education Commission pointed out, "The campaigns were too limited in scale to achieve a significant advance and generate enthusiasm for further effort. They also tended to be sporadic and uncoordinated – government departments, voluntary agencies, educational institutions and individuals working more in isolation than in active collaboration with other agencies. They were often launched hastily, without the careful assessment of the needs and interests of adults, without awakening public interest or stimulating the desire to learn and without adequate provision for the follow-up work in the absence of which no lasting results could be obtained. It is, therefore, not surprising that they failed."[96] Highlighting the importance of literacy in the context of efforts made by the government since Independence, the Education Commission pointed out, "Illiteracy among the masses is inconsistent with the spirit of the age in which scientific and technical progress determines the way of life and standards of living. New ideas and new practices cannot be effectively communicated to minds which are untrained to receive them and to make use of them. Whether it is family planning or improvement of sanitary standards or any programme of social security or any move which requires change of attitude and habits of life, it must make sense to the people."[97] The Education Commission expressed its views on participation and democracy in the rural areas in the context of Panchayati Raj thus: "it should be realised that uneducated people cannot make a real democracy, the essence of which lies in participation by the people in organised civic life and in important decision-making."[98]

However, the programme of adult education started in real earnest during 1978. The primary focus of this progamme was eradication of illiteracy through NGOs by providing grants. For this purpose, part time instructors were recruited and paid a modest honorarium. However, within 10 years of its beginning, the programme fizzled out due to structural deficiencies, inflexibility in approach, inadequacy of funds, attitudinal problems in the bureaucracy, lack of credible voluntary organizations, etc."[99]

This approach was replaced by the total literacy campaign in 1988. Reliance was put on both voluntary organisations, and social action groups. However, there was one difference, it was time-bound, and campaigns involved a number of social partners through the creation of district literacy societies. It has been reported that, by 1993, this programme also came to a halt because of faulty planning and lack of continuity of policies which led to the demise of an otherwise exciting process.[100]

Similarly, the new literacy mission, set up in 1988 with the target of making 100 million persons in the age group of 15-35 literate in a phased manner, also faced with some difficulties specially in the low literacy states mainly due to the absence of voluntary organisations and other socio-cultural barriers. It was further pointed out in the Mid Term Appraisal of Ninth Five Year Plan (1997-2002) that, "There is growing awareness that the Continuing Education Programme requires a qualitative upgradation in order to make it relevant, contextual and acceptable."[101]

In the background of the above, it has been pointed out: "The education system of today, therefore, continues to support, as in the pre-independence days, domination of the privileged groups and domestication or co-opting of the under-privileged ones and does not support liberating forces to the required extent. This situation will not change unless we take vigorous steps to provide genuine political education on an adequate scale. This is one of the major educational reforms we need; and if it is not carried out, mere linear expansion of the existing system of formal education will only support the status quo and hamper radical social transformation."[102]

Political Education

However, there is another side of the picture especially in the context of political education. As a part of the struggle for political freedom, "the Indian people did manage to get a political education which, in the long run, helped them to win freedom. This happened outside the school system, in the freedom struggle which Gandhiji organised. Here, the people participated in millions and got political education through personal involvement, a case of 'learning by doing'. Gandhiji was, therefore, the best exponent of non-formal education the country has ever had and India after Gandhiji was vastly different from the India before him. It was the 'political literacy' he spread among even the people that enabled us to become a sovereign democratic republic."[103]

It is also important to mention here that the Nationalist Movement in India in the early 1920s broadened the base of leadership from relatively small English educated and westernised leaders to a more popular movement with people drawn from medium and small towns, people from lower castes and from rural background.[104]

However, in the context of panchayati raj representatives, the expression literacy has to be understood not merely the three R's but it should provide the individual with knowledge, skills and attitudes which will help him..to show a greater and more intelligent participation in civic life. In the context of adult education, it has to be emphasised that the Constitution defines a person adult above the age of 18 years as adult who has voting right. However, no provision was made in the Constitution for adult education. As a result, no priority was given to adult education and it is not surprising that we have more than 1/3rd of our population as illiterate.

Besides, the social education programme in the community development was an important component. However, since the beginning, there was a lot of confusion about the role and the functions of Social Education Organisers (SEO). The 6th Development Commissioner's Conference defined the role of social education organiser in the following words: "various aspects of social education which will help bring about a change in the outlook of the people; create an urge for better living; organise the people through the formation of community institutions; educate the public about the implications and essentials of planning, about their rights, duties and obligations as citizens; inculcate an interest about the knowledge of the country; organise cultural and recreational activities as also promote education and adult education."[105]

In the absence of any definite improvement, it was recommended that the village teachers should be brought in social educational aspect. It was emphasized that the village teachers be provided two months training in methods of extension, principles of social education and cooperation, and the ideology and methodology of community programme. The Second Five Year Plan also recognized this need and pointed out: "rapid, social and economic progress along democratic lines and widespread illiteracy are scarcely compatible with each other."[106] Balvantray Mehta Committee was critical of the fact that there has not been significant progress in adult literacy work despite the fact that it has been an important part of community development programme. Similarly, United Nations Community Development Evaluation Mission in 1959, pointed out that the social education organisers are entrusted with the "most vital and delicate task of training village leaders" However, it was felt by the Mission that they had no clear idea regarding "what the groups are for; what activities they are likely, or are intended, to take up; and how such new groups coalesce with, differ from, or present challenges to, existing groups in the villages."[107]

The Social Education Organiser also had the responsibility of this work in nearly 100 villages which was again a difficult task. In fact, this task was far beyond the capacity of the majority of social education organisers. In a way it was a very frustrating activity and which did not give them esteem and confidence of other block officials. It is also interesting to point out that teaching adults about citizenship and democracy besides some instruction in elementary economics of development was beyond their capacity. The UN mission further pointed out that it was difficult for Social Education Organisers to work out of this kind of programme. On social education in the Balwantray Mehta Committee there was a "Minute of Dissent by B.G. Rao" primarily on the point that there was no need for a separate and specific organisation for the purpose of social education. He was also critical of the fact that the building up of local leadership has been conceived "on wrong lines". "The leaders in a democratic country grow and are not grown."[108] He went to the extent of pointing out that "Social Education Organiser is not an essential part of the community development organisation."[109]

Political education and political literacy has been subjects of great significance even in the western countries in the context of education for citizenship. The expression 'political literacy' has been defined as "the knowledge, skills and attitudes needed to make a man or women informed about politics; able to participate in public life and groups of all kinds, both occupational and voluntary, and to recognise the tolerate diversities of political and social values.[110] Naik has defined political education "as the preparation of a citizen to take well-informed, responsible, and sustained action for participation in the national struggle for their realisation of the socio-economic objectives of the country.[111] He further pointed out that political education, like any other education, involves: "imparting essential information; building up needed skills to react to or solve problems that arise in day-to-day situations in real life by using the knowledge acquired; and cultivating the needed interests, attitudes and values."[112]

Looking at the complexities involved in terms of number also, it is not possible to provide this education for the elected Panchayati Raj representatives. Therefore, some kind of non-formal system of education or training is suggested for them.

REFERENCES

1. Mill, John Stuart. 1861. Considerations on Representative Government, in *Essays on Politics and Society,* Vol. 19 of *Collected Works,* Editor of the Text J.M. Robson. London: Routledge and Kegan Paul.1977. pp. 534-545.
2. Ibid. p. 534.
3. Ibid. p. 542.
4. Ibid. p. 540.
5. Mill, John Stuart. 1824-1845. *Essays on Economics and Society,* Vol. 4 of *Collected Works,* Textual Editor J.M. Robson. London: Routledge and Kegan Paul. 1967. pp. 363-389.
6. Mill, John Stuart. 1850-1879. *Essays on Economics and Society,* Vol. 5 of *Collected Works,* Textual Editor J.M. Robson. London: Routledge and Kegan Paul. 1967. p. 713.
7. Ibid. p. 727.
8. Rowntree, B. Seebohm. n.d. *Poverty: A Study Of Town Life.* London: Thomas Nelson & Sons.
9. Ibid. p. 166.
10. Ibid. pp. 353-354.
11. Mill, John Stuart. 1861. Considerations on Representative Government, op. cit. p. 536.
12. Mill, John Stuart. 1824-1845. Essays on Economics and Society, Vol. 4. *op. cit.* p. 377.
13. Ibid. p. 377.
14. Ibid. p. 377.
15. Ibid. p. 377.
16. Ibid. p. 375.
17. Ibid. p. 370.
18. Ibid. p. 370.
19. Mill, John Stuart. 1848. *Principles of Political Economy with Some of Their Applications to Social Philosophy.* Books III-V. Vol. 3 of Collected Works, Textual Editor J.M. Robson. London: Routledge & Kegan Paul, 1965. p. 763. See also Longrod,

Georges, 1953. Local Government and Democracy. Public Administration (London). Vol. 31, Sping. Pp. 30-32; Wilson, C.H. (ed.). 1948. Essays on Local Government. Oxford: Basil Blackwell. Pp. 16-21. and Hill, Dilys M. 1974. Democratic Theory and Local Government. London: George Allen and Unwin Ltd. P.28.

20. Mill, John Stuart. 1824-1845. Essays on Economics and Society, Vol. 4. *op. cit.* p. 375.
21. Simon, Brian. 1960. *Studies In The History Of Education 1780-1870.* London: Lawrence & Wishart. pp. 126-176 and 223-276.
22. Ibid. p. 168.
23. Ibid. p. 168.
24. Mill, John Stuart. 1824-1845. Essays on Economics and Society, Vol. 4. *op. cit.* pp. 378-379.
25. Garforth, F. W. 1980. *Educative Democracy: John Stuart Mill on Education in Society*. New York: Oxford University Press. p. 36.
26. Ibid. p. 47.
27. Garforth, F.W. 1980. Educative Democracy: John Stuart Mill on Education in Society. New York: Oxford University Press. p. 48. See also Redlich, Josef and Eranics W. Hirst. 1958. The History of Local Government in England. Being a Reissue of Book 1 of Local Government in England. Edited with Introduction and Epilogue by Bryan Keith – Lucas. London: Macmillan and Co. Ltd. Pp. 195-196.
28. Bryce, James. 1921. *Modern Democracies Vol. II.* London: Macmillan And Co., Limited. pp. 545-568.
29. Ibid. p. 554.
30. Ibid. p. 556.
31. Ibid. p. 565.
32. India. Indian Statutory Commission Volume 1.1930. *Report of the Indian Statutory Commission Volume 1–Survey.* London: HMSO. p. 298.
33. Gopal, S. 1965. British Policy in India. 1858-1905. Cambridge: Cambridge University Press. p.93. See also S. Gopal. 1953. The Viceroyalty of Lord Ripon 1880-1884. London: Oxford University Press. pp. 83-112.
34. Quoted in Wickwar, W. Hardy. 1970. *the political theory of local government*. columbia, south carolina: university of south carolina press. p. 25.
35. Misra, B. B. 1970. *The Administrative History of India 1834-1947.* New Delhi: Oxford University Press. p. 602.
36. Ibid. p. 602.

37. Ibid. p. 602.
38. Ibid. p. 603.
39. Ibid. p. 603.
40. Ibid. p. 603.
41. Ibid. p. 604.
42. India. *Report of The Royal Commission Upon Decentralization In India,* Vol. 1. 1909. London: HMSO. p. 269.
43. Ibid. p. 269.
44. *Speeches of Gopal Krishna Gokhale.* 1916. Second Edition. Madras: G. A. Natesan & Co. p. 1213.
45. Ibid. p. 674.
46. Ibid. p. 1010.
47. Ibid. p. 1012.
48. Ibid. p. 851.
49. Ibid. p. 1054.
50. Ibid. pp. 1054-1055.
51. Ibid. p. 837.
52. Quoted in Tinker, Hugh. 1954. *The Foundations of Local Self-Government in India, Pakistan and Burma.* London: Athlone Press. p. 112.
53. Ibid. pp. 336 and 343.
54. Haynes, Douglas E. 1992. *Rhetoric and Ritual in Colonial India: The Shaping of a Public Culture in Surat City, 1852-1928.* New Delhi: Oxford University Press. p. 173.
55. India. Constitution Assembly Debates. 1948. Ambedkar, B.R. *Statement in the Constituent Assembly of India on the Motion re. Draft Constitution.* 4th November, 7(1). Government of India Press. New Delhi. p. 39.
56. India. Constitution Assembly Debates. 1948. Das, Monomohan. *Statement in the Constituent Assembly of India on the Motion re. Draft Constitution.* 8thNovember, 7(4). Government of India Press. New Delhi. p. 308.
57. India. Constitution Assembly Debates. 1949. Misra, Lokanath. *Statement in the Constituent Assembly of India on the Motion re. Draft Constitution.* 22nd November, 11(8). Government of India Press. New Delhi. p. 798.
58. India. Constitution Assembly Debates. 1949. Wilson, T.J.M. *Statement in the Constituent Assembly of India on the Motion re. Draft Constitution.* 23rd November, 11(9). Government of India Press. New Delhi. p. 857.
59. India. Committee on Plan Projects. 1957. *Report of the Team For The Study of Community Projects And National Extension Service,*

Vol. 1. New Delhi. (Chairman: Balvantray G. Mehta). p. 23.
60. Narayan. Jayaprakash. 1970. Communitarian Society and Panchayati Raj. Edited with an Introduction by Brahmanand. Varanasi: Navchetna. Prakashan. Pp. 75-76.
61. Ibid. p. 87.
62. India. Ministry of Agriculture And Irrigation, Department of Rural Development. 1978. *Report of The Committee on Panchayati Raj Institutions*. New Delhi. (Chairman: Asoka Mehta). pp. 6-7.
63. Ibid. pp. 156-170.
64. India. Ministry of Agriculture, Department of Rural Development. 1985. *Report of The Committee To Review The Existing Administrative Arrangements For Rural Development And Poverty Alleviation Programmes*, New Delhi, (Chairman: G.V.K. Rao), p. 41.
65. India. Ministry of Agriculture, Department of Rural Development. 1986. *A Draft Concept Paper on Revitalisation of Panchayati Raj Institutions For Democracy And Development* by Committee For the Concept Paper on Panchayati Raj Institutions. New Delhi. (Chairman: L. M. Singhvi). p. 14.
66. Jain, L. C., B. V. Krishnamurthy and P. M. Tripathi.1985. *Grass Without Roots: Rural Development Under Government Auspices*. New Delhi: Sage. p. 217.
67. Quoted in Bandyopadhyay, D. 1997. People's Participation in Planning: Kerala Experiment. *Economic and Political Weekly*, 32(39), 27 September. p. 2451.
68. Quoted in Mohan Lal, G. Morley. 1994. *Rajiv Gandhi and Panchayati Raj: Democracy and Development at the Grassroots*. Delhi: Konark Publishers. p. 19.
69. G. Venkat Swamy. Minister of State in the Ministry of Rural Development, Department of Rural Development moving a Resolution on Panchayati Raj in the Parliament on 1st December, 1992 quoted in Rajiv Gandhi Foundation, National Workshop on Panchayati Raj. May 19-20, 1993. pp. 14-22.
70. Ibid. p. 20.
71. Vyasulu, Poornima and Vinod Vyasulu. 1999. Women in Panchayati Raj Grass Roots Democracy in Malgudi. *Economic and Political Weekly*, 34(52), 25 December. p.3684., and Bidyut Mohanty. 1995. Panchayati Raj, 73rd Constitutional Amendment and Women. *Economic and Political Weekly*, 30(52), 30 December. pp. 3346-3350.
72. Pai, Sudha. 1998. Pradhanis in New Panchayats: Field Notes from Meerut District. *Economic and Political Weekly*, 33(18), 2

May. p.1010.

73. Mathew, George and Ramesh C. Nayak, 1996. Panchayats at Work: What It Means for the Oppressed? *Economic and Political Weekly*, 31(27), 6 July. p.1771.
74. Beteille, Andre. 1999. Empowerment. *Economic and Political Weekly*, 34(10&11), 6-13 March. pp. 595-596.
75. Ibid. p.597.
76. Verba, Sidney. 1967. Democratic Participation. *The Annals*, Vol. 373, September. p.63.
77. Haynes, Douglas E. *op. cit.* p. 149.
78. Sathyamurthy, T. V. 1995. Panchayat Raj and India's Two Societies. Review Article. *Economic and Political Weekly*, 30(3), 21 January. p.156.
79. Ibid. p. 156.
80. Pai, Sudha. 2001. Social Capital, Panchayats and Grass Roots Democracy Politics of Dalit Assertion in Uttar Pradesh. *Economic and Political Weekly*, 36(8), 24 February. p.652.
81. Lieten, G. K. and Ravi Srivastava. 1999. *Unequal Partners: Power Relations, Devolution and Development in Uttar Pradesh*. New Delhi: Sage. p. 266.
82. Ibid. p. 265.
83. RoyChowdhury Supriya. 2002. Behind every 'successful' woman. *The Hindu*, 21 April. P. 16.
84. Ibid. pp. 16-17.
85. Ibid. p. 17.
86. Quoted in Datta Prabhat and Panchali Bhattacharyya Sen. 2000. Participatory Rural Governance in India. *Indian Journal of Public Administration*, 46(1), January -March. p. 46.
87. Ibid. p. 46.
88. David L. Sills (Editor). 1968. International Encyclopedia of the Social Sciences. Vol. 12. The Macmillan Company and the Free Press. p. 258.
89. Ibid. p. 255.
90. Naik, J. P. 1977. *Some Perspectives on Non-Formal Education*. New Delhi: Allied. pp.79-80.
91. Nurullah, Syed and J. P. Naik. 1951. *A History of Education In India. (During the British Period)*. Second Edition. Bombay: Macmillan & Co. Ltd. P.813.
92. Citizens For Democracy. 1978. *Education for Our People: A Policy Frame for the Development of Education over the Next Ten Years (1978-87)*. New Delhi: Allied. p.11.
93. Myrdal, Gunnar. 1982. *Asian Drama: An Inquiry Into the Poverty*

of Nations, Vol. III. New Delhi: Kalyani. p.1656.

94. Quoted in Myrdal, Gunnar. 1970. *The Challenge of World Poverty: A World Anti-Poverty Program in Outline*. London: Penguin Books. p.184.
95. India. Ministry of Education. 1967. *Report of The Education Commission 1964-66. Education and National Development*. p. 423.
96. Ibid. p. 424.
97. Ibid. p. 424.
98. Ibid. p. 424.
99. Ramachandran, Vimla. 1999. Adult Education: A Tale of Empowerment Denied. *Economic and Political Weekly,* 34(15), 10 April. P. 877.
100. Ibid. . 879.
101. India. Planning Commission. 2000. *Mid Term Appraisal of Ninth Five Year Plan (1997-2002)*. October. New Delhi. p. 202.
102. Naik, J. P. *op. cit.* pp. 81-82.
103. Naik, J. P. *Op. cit.* p.80.
104. Brown, Judith M. 1972. *Gandhi's Rise To Power, Indian Politics 1915-22*. Cambridge: Cambridge University Press. pp. 355-356.
105. India. Committee on Plan Projects. 1957. *Report of the Team For The Study of Community Projects And National Extension Service,* Vol. 1. *op. cit.* p. 102.
106. Ibid. p.105.
107. India. Ministry of Community Development and Co-operation, Department of Community Development. 1959. *Report of A Community Development Evaluation Mission In India*. New Delhi. p.56.
108. India. Committee on Plan Projects. *op. cit.* p. 123.
109. Ibid. p. 124.
110. Crick, Bernard and Alex Porter (ed.). 1978. Political Education and Political Literacy, London: Longman. P.1.
111. Naik, J.P. op. cit. P.82.
112. Ibid. p. 82.

3

Training of Elected Panchayati Raj Representatives: 1959-2006

THE EARLY EXPERIENCE: 1959-1969

In the early 1950s, at the time of the commencement of Community Development Programme (CDP), the training of government functionaries was given a lot of importance. The CDP basically aimed at the economic, political, social and cultural regeneration of the rural areas of the country. The first Prime Minister of India, Jawaharlal Nehru epitomised the essence and importance of training in community development in the following words: "Training is necessary in whatever field of activity one may be engaged in. It is more necessary in Community Development where our aim is to build up the human material, to bring about a change in the spirit of the individual, to make better men and women and to teach them self-reliance and confidence in themselves."[1]

The Union Ministry of Community Development and Cooperation, since 1952, started the programme of training: block development officers, extension officers, social education organisers and the village level workers. This training soon spread to higher echelons of trainer's training and district panchayat officers training at Rajpura, (Dehradun) and the Central Institute of Study and Research, Mussoorie, for the training of officials ranging from collectors to secretaries and development commissioners. All this training was for officials, by trained officials, in established institutions and according to the syllabi prepared by experts.

However, in 1957, the Study Team, set up by the Committee on Plan Projects and presided over by Balvantray Mehta stated: "Democracy has to function through certain executive machinery, but the democratic government operating over large areas through its executive machinery cannot adequately appreciate local needs and circumstances. It is, therefore, necessary that there should be a devolution of power and a decentralisation of machinery and that such power be exercised and such machinery controlled and directed by popular representatives of the local area."[2] Introduction of Panchayat Raj (PR) in 1959 involved the people and their representatives more directly in the community. The implementation of the CDP and fulfilment of targets was as much a responsibility of the extension agency as that of the people. In the new set-up of panchayati raj, people's representatives were to govern their own affairs over a fairly large field. It was presumed that great responsibility rested upon popular representatives after the devolution of local development sector on PRIs. As such, they were to represent the wishes of the constituents, take major decisions, find resources for carrying out the decisions, etc. It meant the people's representatives were also to be helped in their work through suitable orientation programmes. It became necessary to train not only the officials but also a large number of non-officials – the *panches, sarpanches, pradhans and pramukhs* to enable them to govern their own affairs and to formulate plans for the integrated development of their area. In the training courses for community development workers, therefore, an increasing number of non-officials were brought in and suitable adjustments in the syllabi, etc., were made to meet their requirements.

The objectives of the various training programmes were as follows:

- To ensure that both officials and non-officials get a common understanding of the philosophy, objectives and methods of CDP.
- Both officials and non-officials acquire knowledge of methods of working with people.

- The officials in particular learn techniques and skills to enable them to impart useful knowledge and information to people during the course of Extension Work.
- Both officials and non-officials develop an understanding of each other's role so as to establish a harmonious working relationship among themselves.[3]

Advisory Board on Training

At the national level in 1960, an Advisory Board on Training, consisting of some Members of Parliament, officials and a few others, was constituted to organize, supervise and guide the policy and the broad pattern of official and non-official training. The Board was expected to review the progress of the programme, and suggest modifications or alterations. Three Committees of the Advisory Board on Training were constituted in order to deal with the following subjects: Central Institute of Study and Research in Community Development; Orientation and Study Centres and other Training Centres at the national and state levels and Study and Orientation Programme at the district level and below. The Board was reconstituted as a National Council for Study and Research in Community Development and Panchayati Raj in June, 1962 with enlarged functions and responsibilities. The Council consisted of Members of Parliament, other important non-officials and officials represented the various Ministries of the Government of India and the State Governments. The National Council had set up a Standing Committee with a Vice-Chairman nominated by Government and three functional committees. State governments were also requested to set up similar committees.[4]

Magnitude of the Task

The programme of training envisaged covering 16 lakh *panches*, 2 lakh *sarpanches*, 2 lakhs *up-sarpanches*, 5000 *pradhans*, 325 *pramukhs*. Besides, nearly 300 members of the sub-committees of different State Legislatures and over 100 MPs serving on various committees and sub-committees of the Parliament and

State Legislatures dealing with the training programme for community development were to be given special training. Facilities for study and orientation were also to be provided for much larger number of youth leaders, women workers, selected gram sahayaks – in fact, the entire adult population of 200 million or members of Gram Sabhas at that point of time.[5]

The objectives of the training could be summed up as follows:

- To help Panchayats to draw up plan and fix priorities according to the village needs and resources.
- To foster spirit of cooperation in the village.
- To prepare people to adopt new methods of agricultural production, credit, marketing and village industries.
- To mobilise people for the execution of the plan.
- To instil in the minds of the people, faith and the spirit of self-help.[6]

Training Programmes

A number of training programmes were developed for the non-officials under the panchayati raj set-up. Some of the broad categories of these programmes are given below:

MPs and MLAs

For the members of Lok Sabha and Vidhan Sabhas, a three-fold programme of education and orientation was evolved. At the National level, an Informal Consultative Committee of the Members of Parliament, (both the Houses), was constituted. State Governments were also requested to set up similar committees, comprising of members of the State Legislatures. State Governments were further requested to co-opt Members of the Central Informal Consultative Committee also. These committees were expected to review the progress of the programme, and suggest modifications or alterations as and when necessary. They were requested to attend as many district meetings as possible. It was also expected that they should form study circles of MPs and MLAs and discuss the programme of community development. They were required to participate in village leaders' camps and educate people in the philosophy of community development. A sub-committee on training and education was set up to advise the Union Ministry of Community Development on the policy and broad pattern of official and non-official training. Similar educational and training sub-committees of the Informal Consultative Committee were being recommended for the states also. The state governments organised study camps for MPs and MLAs. These provided an opportunity for exchange of views on the community development programme. The MPs and MLAs were also invited to participate in the orientation courses at the Central Institute of Study and Research in Community Development, Mussoorie.

Members of Zila Parishad/Pramukhs

The members were provided study and orientation facilities in community development at the Central Institute of Study and Research in Community Development, Mussoorie, which conducted one month's course for officials and non-officials. Broadly, they were given orientation in the following subjects: philosophy and the dynamics of the community development programme, planning and executing agriculture, animal husbandry, irrigation programmes, etc.

Members of Block Development Committees/Panchayat Samitis

For the training of non-official members of block development committees and members of panchayat samitis, an elaborate scheme was launched during 1959-60. This scheme consisted of two phases. In the first phase, training was provided to the trainers. These trainers were selected by the state governments and sent for two week's training to the camps, which were organised by the Union Government. These centres were established at New Delhi, Hyderabad, Jabalpur and Ranchi. In all, 208 persons, nominated by the state governments were given training for two weeks. The second phase consisted of training of non-official members of block development committees and members of panchayat samitis. The state governments, through non-official organizations, implemented it with financial assistance from the Union Government. A ceiling was prescribed under which per capita cost of training was kept within Rs.50/-. It was proposed that all the members of the panchayat samitis, approximately 1,50,000 members may be trained by the end of 1963. The training of non-officials of block development committee was taken up in 1959 in all states except Jammu & Kashmir and Madras (Tamil Nadu). The states of West Bengal and Andhra Pradesh conducted these training programmes through peripatetic teams. The duration of such training programmes varied between 2-10 days.

The syllabus for the training was prepared by a Syllabus Committee of Members of Parliament under the Chairmanship of Balvantray Mehta.[7] The broad contents of the syllabus included: local self-government institutions and their role in the process of democratic decentralisation; district planning with emphasis on the block plan; duties and rights of public representatives; sarvodaya; philosophy and objectives of CDP; the role of peoples' representatives in the programmes; implementation of the CDP; and know your village. This syllabus also covered practical field visits and study tours to institutions like: panchayat; cooperative society; cooperative bank and agricultural related institutions, block headquarters, district headquarters, district banks and cooperative marketing societies. The idea was to understand the processes and working methods of some important institutions.

Sarpanches and Panches

The orientation and Study Programme for *Sarpanches* and Panches had two aspects – camp study and peripatetic training. The camp study was usually for six days. Subjects for discussion came under three main categories – (a) general knowledge, which included topics like: the government, Five Year Plans, philosophy and objective of CDP, three basic primary institutions, the State Panchayat Act, etc. (b) learning basic things about modern methods and techniques of agriculture, animal husbandry, minor irrigation, public health and sanitation, rural housing, industries, etc., and (c) field visits, with a view to educating the non-officials. There was also a scheme for providing study and orientation courses to panches through peripatetic teams consisting of a social education organiser, a block level panchayat officer, an outstanding *gram sevak* and two non-officials. The team was constituted by the block panchayat samiti. This peripatetic team held camps in each of the *gram sevak's* circle for about three days. This scheme was financed from block development budget to the extent of Re.1 per head per day. The training of panches in the camps was organised in the states of Assam, Bihar, Punjab, Gujarat, Maharashtra, Madhya Pradesh, Rajasthan and Uttar Pradesh. About 2,41,478 panches were trained in these states.[8]

For the training of sarpanches, up-sarpanches, panches, members of block development committees/panchayat samities, etc., sanction was issued for setting up 50 Panchayat Raj Training Centres (PRTCs) in 1961-62 and another such 50 institutions in 1962-63. It was also decided to make the training of sarpanches, up-sarpanches and block development committee members institutional (in courses of one week duration). Training of panches was conducted in camps of three days duration through the peripatetic teams of the PRTCs. The following safeguards were laid down for selection of non-official organisations taking up training programmes:

- The non-official agency should be in general agreement with the philosophy and objectives of community development and Panchayati Raj.
- The prescribed syllabus is covered in full, in case of each category of non-officials.
- Training should be imparted in as objective a manner as possible.
- The non-official organisation should present an objective picture of the policies and programmes of the Government.[9]

Syllabus for the Training of Sarpanches, Upsarpanches and Panches was divided into the following categories:[10]

- General Knowledge: The objective was to create proper approach, attitudes, initiative and leadership by informed talks and discussions on planning, civic duties, philosophy and objectives of community development; the State Panchayat Act and the Rules made thereunder;

- Technical Subjects: The objective was to impart basic knowledge of modern methods and techniques in public health and sanitation, agriculture, animal husbandry, minor irrigation, rural housing and industries. Besides talks and discussions, this programme also included field demonstrations.
- Field Visits: The objective was educational visits to institutions.

However, it was made clear that the state governments were free to adopt either of the two pattern of training to suit local conditions. It was also decided that the training centres should preferably be run by non-officials agencies which have already been running similar programmes and have a good record of service in rural areas. Where such non-official agencies are not available, the zila parishad be entrusted to conduct these programmes. The non-official organisations running the PRTCs were left free in the matter of day-to-day administration. However, overall supervision of the training programmes of the PRTCs was done by a managing committee which consisted of representatives of zila parishads, agency running the Panchayati Raj Centre and the state government. By 1961-62, nearly 100 training centres were set up in the country.[11] Approximately 79,000 elected representatives received training at these centres during 1964-65.[12]

A committee, headed by G. Ramachandran, M.P. and comprising of Members of Parliament and other experts, was set up in 1964 to evaluate the working of PRTCs. In the light of the recommendations made by the committee, in 1967, the question of strengthening the existing PRTCs, (after their numbers have been readjusted to ensure optimum utilisation), was examined in consultation with the state governments. Expenditure on PRTCs from 1968-69 was incurred entirely by the state governments concerned. Due to the paucity of resources, several states decided to close a number of these institutions.

Sammelans

During 1961-62, a scheme for organising sammelans for non-officials at village, block, district and state levels was sanctioned and comprehensive instructions issued to the state governments for implementation. The purpose was the training of non-officials through exchange of ideas. Under this scheme, central assistance was made available only for the state level sammelans on ad-hoc basis to the extent of Rs.50/- per head, subject to the overall ceiling in respect of each state. For sammelans at lower levels, the state governments were requested to find funds from local contributions or their own resources. These sammelans were organised at least once in a year at each level.

Training of Trainers

A programme of study and orientation for trainers preferably through non-official organisations like the *Bharat Sevak Samaj, Harijan Sevak Samaj, Kasturba Trust, Gandhi Smarak Nidhi,* etc., was also undertaken. Representatives of social organisations, selected by the state, were given an orientation course for about a month, in special study camps organised by the Ministry of Community Development and Cooperation. These trainers, after an intensive course, used to go back to their state to organise similar camps, in cooperation with the non-official organisations and the state governments and impart similar courses in study and orientation to the workers concerned in the states. Since 1964-65, the new recruits to the staff were deputed to the four and half months courses for instructors at the National Institute of Community Development. In these courses, the instructors were not only trained in teaching methods, but also received theoretical instructions in the basic social sciences. Selected instructors are also deputed for advanced training abroad with the assistance of grants received from the Ford Foundation.

To acquire deeper field insights, the teaching staff at the training centres were expected to take up case-studies and short-term research investigations. They were also encouraged to take part in appropriate workshops and seminars and to contribute papers and articles to professional journals. Apart from these measures, the teaching staff undertook regular study and follow-up tours to obtain first hand knowledge of current developments in the field and to assist through personal contacts with former trainees, the manner and extent of the effectiveness of the training imparted.

Management of Training Programmes

A large number of suggestions about the working of the training programmes of non-officials emanated from the assurances of the Ministry of Community Development and Cooperation.[13] The following suggestions were later on acted by the Ministry:

- The involvement of voluntary organisations of repute in conducting the training programmes.
- The institutions engaged in rural development and in the training of social service and social welfare should also be given preference.
- The Managing Committee of a Panchayati Raj Training Centres should have 5 members: (a representative each of the state government and Zila Parishad, 2 representatives of the organisation running the Centre and the Principal of the Training Centre as Member-Secretary).
- The Managing Committee should meet more frequently and maintain closer touch with the training centres.
- The pattern of financial assistance to the Panchayati Raj Training Centres was also liberalised from January, 1964 by making expenditure on salaries of staff and establishment charges completely independent of attendance.
- The state governments were requested to issue instructions making the Collector, the District Planning Officer and the Block Development Officer responsible for ensuring adequate attendance. The question of attendance was coming up again and again since the inception of these programmes. It was also suggested

that the panchayat samities should be fully involved in ensuring adequate attendance at these centres.

- It was also emphasised that the educational qualifications, laid down for the teaching staff should be strictly enforced and early steps should be taken to replace unqualified personnel. The selection of teaching staff should be made by a State Level Committee consisting of a representative each of the state government, Zila Parishad and the organisation running the Centre. It was also suggested that the members of the teaching staff should be required to execute a bond agreeing to serve the centre at least for a period of 3 years on completion of their training at the Centre for Training and Research in Panchayat Raj. It was also emphasised that the Principal and instructors of the centre should attend another specialised one month course at the National Institute of Community Development in subjects of teaching methods and communications.
- To review the panchayati raj training programme at regular intervals, a State Level Committee under the Chairmanship of the Development Commissioner was set up so as to provide regular assistance and guidance to these centres.
- Close coordination between the Block Organisation and the Training Centres was also suggested, particularly in matters of attendance, guest lectures, and audio-visual aids, etc.
- It was suggested that the Acts, Rules and Procedures governing the functioning of panchayats should be covered in the syllabi. It was also proposed that lecture-cum-discussion method and group discussions, also be included as integral parts of the courses. It was also suggested that each training centre may be equipped with audio-visual aids and full use should be made of such aids. Library at the PRTCs should have adequate number of suitable books. A scheme was formulated for the production of basic publications in arts, science,

religion, culture, etc., for distribution to village libraries. These books were distributed to each community development block at the rate of 20 copies per block for supply to village libraries at the rate of two copies per gram sevak circle.

Progress of Training Programmes

Tables 1, 2 and 3 provide data on the various institutions established for the training of MPs, MLAs, Zila Adhyaksh and various categories of non-officials at the district, block and gram panchayat levels. It also gives the duration of training, persons trained during the year, etc. The Annual Reports of the Union Ministry of Community Development provide these figures only for the years: 1966-67, 1967-68, and 1968-69. One thing which becomes more obvious is the fact that the number of PRTCs for the training of block and village levels non-officials dwindled from 121 during (1966-67) to 73 during (1967-68) and 55 during (1968-69) (Table 3). Training to panches was given by the peripatetic teams. It is also evident from these tables that, by and large, the officials and non-officials were trained together. As a consequence, it is difficult to identify separately the number of officials and non-officials trained during these years. However, in a way the numbers trained were very impressive. For example, in the category of block and village level elected representatives of panchayati raj, it has been claimed that 6,000 members were trained (Table 3). Similarly, in the composite training centres, around 42,000 block development officers, extensions officers and district level non-officials were trained (Table 3). There was also a provision for the training of trainers as well as training of MPs and MLAs and senior officials at the National Institute of Community Development, Mussoorie (Tables 1 and 2). There was perceptible decline in the training activities after 1966-67 primarily due to a severe drought affecting agriculture production. This made the government to take economy measures which to a large extent affected the budgetary allocation in the community development programmes in general and training activities in particular. Simultaneously, it also resulted in the Department of Community Development, Government of India, putting the PRTCs and orientation and study centres/composite training centres at the disposal of the state governments. However, it has to be recognised that a massive effort was made by the Department of Community Development for the training of officials and non-officials engaged in panchayati raj activities and an attempt was made to involve and train the MPs, MLAs as well as the elected panchayati raj representatives. Training Institutions were established at the national, state and district levels on a massive scale where there was none earlier.

Appraisal of the Training Programmes: 1959-1969

The analysis of training of elected panchayati raj representatives in the preceding pages clearly show that it was launched at a hectic pace. In the process a lot of gaps were left. The magnitude of the task was very large and the organisers of the programme became very ambitious in covering, besides elected representatives, a large number of auxiliary leadership of the village, outside the fold of elected representatives. Hurriedly a large number of institutions were established all over the country, primarily to train the officials as well as non-officials. For the village level non-officials, by and large, voluntary organisations were entrusted the work of training. The training programme of this magnitude, undertaken on an all India basis, also needed synchronisation of a number of activities: selection of trainers, training of trainers, selection of voluntary organisations, funds, development of syllabi, production of literature, infrastructural facilities, administrative arrangements, etc. The report of the Community Development Evaluation Mission in India, under the aegis of United Nations, made the following observations on the training programmes: "Probably no single aspect of community development work in India has received more attention than the need for, and the way to carry out, training schemes... Other countries, less advanced than India in establishing a community development movement to raise the standards of living in rural areas, will find the history and development of training schemes in India, even over the short period since the first projects began, of great value in establishing their own schemes."[14]

It is evident from the preceding pages that a good degree of effort had gone into these training programmes. Effort was also made from time to time to ensure that the training programmes were running according to their objectives. But as pointed out earlier, the task was of a very large magnitude, daunting and complex. There was very little experience in this endeavour. In this process, a number of mistakes were committed. The mistakes were bound to occur as the training needs were not determined scientifically. No effort was made to understand the fact that the training programmes are meant, for elected representatives with little or no education (at least this was true at the level of village and intermediate PRIs).

Looking into the context and the background of the trainees, a number of mistakes were identified in the conduct of these programmes. Firstly, it has been pointed out that the training methodology was not suited to the requirements of these programmes. There was over-emphasis to "pump out the subject matter". As a result, there were little opportunities for expressing oneself, for active participation in the class-room and "for acquiring skills needed to carry out the new responsibilities and for individual guidance."[15] Besides, self-learning was not made as one of the essential feature of the training programme. Similarly, it has also been pointed out that the training programme should have adopted methodology which ought to have encouraged problem-centered discussions, supported by audio-visual aids and field demonstrations.[16]

It was pointed out that the syllabus of training was very heavy. In view of the short duration of the courses, the curriculum was regarded as 'formidable' by the team of UN observers. The curriculum was rigid and lacked adaptability to the changing needs. It was also pointed out that the training programmes did not include learning of appropriate skills and attitudes which were needed for new responsibilities: conducting meetings, controlling and coordinating development programmes, supervision and guidance in the working of constituent organs, dealing with factions, professional groups and securing harmonious relationship with officials.[17] It was rightly observed that in the syllabus of training "More care must be taken with regard to what should not be put in, rather than on what is to be put in."[18]

The Orientation and Study Centres and the National Institute of Community Development, provided opportunities for study and orientation for district and higher level personnel. The study and orientation period lasted for a month. The nominees were sponsored by the respective state governments or the Union Ministry of Community Development and Cooperation. The participants constituted a mixed group consisting of MPs, MLAs, Zila Pramukhs, and Pradhans, university teachers, Collectors and regional departmental heads. The participants were divided into syndicate groups on specifically assigned problems. Besides, syndicate studies, lectures were also arranged. However, the syndicate reports presented "systematic narration and summarisation of the material lying in some better known reports and books and a few practical hints... It is not realised that group thinking has its plateaus."[19] No attempt was made to survey the training needs of the participants.

In the beginning, 50 PRTCs were started on ad-hoc and arbitrary basis by 15 to 20 miscellaneous and mostly unknown voluntary organisations. These organisations were selected by the state governments. Almost all of them had little or no experience of imparting training. These organisations took on the work of training because the government was paying Rs.50/- per trainee per course which was not a small amount at that point of time. Prior to 1964, a good number of PRTCs were started in the districts for training of sarpanches and panches for short periods, but it was found that the sarpanches and panches were not attending the training programmes. As the response continued to be poor, these institutions were closed down. Later on, the panchayat samiti presidents were deputed for a fortnight training in the State Institute of Community Development and Panchayati Raj, but the response was not at all satisfactory. The Chairman of Zila Parishads were deputed to the National Institute of Community Development for one month's training but most of them did not attend the training. Poor attendance of block development committee members in almost all the training centres was also noticed. It was also reported that this was to a great extent due to the inefficient and inadequate running of PRTCs. It was also pointed out that, both in PRTCs and peripatetic training programmes, there used to be no attempt to suit the convenience of the trainees. The training centres were situated in urban or semi-urban areas rather than in rural areas and were devoid of the natural surroundings.

With the decline of importance of the community development programme in the late sixties and along with the fact that these institutions were suffering from a number of problems, the PRTCs, by and large, in a large number of states became defunct bodies.[20] In fact, the Vengal Rao Committee in Andhra Pradesh recommended that all such training centres should be abolished and panchayati raj training programmes should be wound up. But, at the same time, Sadiq Ali Committee in Rajasthan and Narasimhan Committee in Andhra Pradesh recommended that all office bearers of PRIs should undergo prescribed training courses within a stipulated period from the date of their assuming office for the first time. Both these committees also recommended that failure to undergo the training within this stipulated period should be a disqualification for their continuing to hold office. These committees also recommended that, for the period of training, suitable training allowances should be paid to the non-officials.

It was also observed that it was difficult to get the instructors who had considerable field experience along with knowledge in the theory of work. By and large, most of the instructors lacked the balance between grounding in theory and experience in field programme. As a result (in the later years), the government decided to select instructors on deputation.[21] The instructors also lacked the urge and discipline to study.

A number of flaws were noticed in the training programmes. The selection of instructors was made by state governments in some cases and by voluntary organisations in other cases. It was also noticed that out of a large number of instructors trained, many of them did not work in these training programmes. As such, there was a lot of wastage. Secondly, the instructors selected were not fit for imparting such training. In fact, it was reported that, from the point of view of suitability, 80-90 per cent were unfit for this type of work. Most of these instructors were selected casually without any clear understanding about their academic qualifications, experience and social service background, etc.[22] Most of such persons who joined as instructors were retired persons or social workers with little idea about the type of responsibilities which they had to shoulder. The instructors were paid between Rs. 50 to Rs.100 per course as a weekly wage and then used to be discharged.

Regarding the PRTCs, it has been rightly summed up "The training centres could not outgrow their narrow departmentalistic ways of thinking. There were few linkages, if any, with the wider educational stream. The capacities of the centres were under-utilised. Some staff lacked strength in theory while others did not have the firm grasp of field situations. The libraries were poorly equipped. The teaching was stereotyped. The education was too heterogeneous. In certain fields, discontinuities in policies created confusion. The organisation of village practicals defied a satisfactory solution."[23]

PANCHAYATI RAJ TRAINING: 1970-2006

The role of the Union Ministry of Rural Development (formerly known as the Union Ministry of Community Development, Cooperation and Panchayati Raj, later renamed as Department of Community Development) in the organisation of training programmes was prominent during the days of community development. In 1967-68, all the training institutions, known as Orientation and Study Centres, which were till then directly managed and controlled by the Union Government, were transferred to the states and renamed as State Institutes of Community Development/Panchayati Raj. Recently, some have been renamed as State Institutes of Rural Development.

A scheme was introduced during the Sixth Five Year Plan with a view to strengthening the state institutes for training and research in rural development. The scheme envisaged the establishment, of new institutions as also the strengthening of the existing ones. In the first phase, it was proposed to strengthen one state level institute in each state. It was also proposed to provide 50 per cent of the recurring and non-recurring expenditure as central grant-in-aid. The balance 50 per cent was to be met by the concerned state government. In the case of North East States and Sikkim, the Union Government provided 100 per cent assistance on non-recurring items also. The Central share for non-recurring items such as the construction of hostels was limited to Rs. 5 lakh per institute and its share on non-recurring items came to Rs. 1 lakh per year and limited to Rs. 5 lakh per institute. An outlay of Rs.125 lakh was provided in the Sixth Plan towards the scheme. By 1982-83, nine institutions were assisted with necessary grants, involving an expenditure of Rs. 31.42 lakh.

It is evident from the above that since the First Five Year Plan and the commencement of community development programme in 1952 as well as the commencement of panchayati raj in the early sixties, led to a considerable growth of training infrastructure at the state level. Table-4 shows the state-wise number of training institutions like Administrative Training Institutions (ATIs), State Institute of Rural Development (SIRD), as well as lower level training institutions which are classified as Extension Training Centres (ETCs) and Farmers Training Centres (FTCs). However, it is necessary to point out that administrative training institutions in some of the states like Gujarat, Himachal Pradesh, Jammu and Kashmir, Karnataka, Maharashtra, Rajasthan, Tripura and Manipur are composite training institutions i.e. these institutions combine both administrative training and rural development training for the field functionaries. In some of the states, primarily in Uttar Pradesh, there are institutions at the state level dealing with planning and management also. Besides, at the lower level, almost all the states are having extension training centres and farmers training centres. The number varies from each state depending on the size and the requirements of the concerned state.

At the state level, as on date, there are around 288 institutions both in the higher and lower categories which are catering to the needs of the rural development. At the apex level is National Institute of Rural Development, Hyderabad which is primarily responsible at the national level for conducting research and training in rural development and related areas. Besides, there are other institutions which conduct both research and training in the areas of rural development, district planning, democratic decentralization, etc. Some of these institutions are: Indian Institute of Public Administration, New Delhi; National Academy of Administration, Mussoorie, All India Institute of Local Self Government, Mumbai; and Institute for Social and Economic Change, Bangalore.

The Constitution (Seventy-third) Amendment Act, 1992, was brought into force with effect from. 24th April, 1993. The Ministry of Rural Development, Government of India initiated a process of training of elected panchayati raj representatives. In this connection, the Prime Minister of India, P.V. Narasimha Rao, in July 1993 in his inaugural address at the Conference of Ministers and Secretaries of Panchayats of States and Union Territories, highlighted the need for training of elected panchayati raj representatives, "Since a large number of members will be coming from the weaker sections of the society, it will be necessary to give them comprehensive training about their roles, responsibilities and overall philosophy behind these PRIs. They have to know the procedures, rules and working of the Government and these local institutions to effectively discharge the roles assigned to them. This training should not be a one-time affair and should be conducted at regular intervals for continuous updating of knowledge and skills. States should take stock of the situation and make provisions for the training of Panchayati Raj functionaries, both official and non-official. The Ministry of Rural Development has also been working on evolving a comprehensive training programme for the functionaries and will suitably assist the States in their efforts."[24] One of the major recommendations of the Conference was regarding training to all functionaries involved in the Panchayat Raj system at every level. In order to do this, the existing Panchayati Raj training centres at different levels require to be revitalised and strengthened in their capabilities.[25]

IIPA Workshop

Another major highlight in the initial phase was a workshop titled Strategy for Training Under New Panchayati Raj, organised by the Indian Institute of Public Administration, New Delhi on 30th July, 1993. The objectives of the seminar were to: examine the administrative and financial implications of training and suggest appropriate measures for timely completion of training programme in an effective manner; identify state-wise training institutions in the light of requirements of training for different categories of trainees, both non-officials and officials at different levels; suggest measures for strengthening of training infrastructure; and develop training modules for national level Training of Trainers (TOT) programme in the light of training needs to be identified at the Workshop and to specify the trainees for the same e.g. from Administrative Training Institute, State Institute of Rural Development, University system and development departments etc.[26]

Some of the important recommendations of the workshop are given below.

- Training is quite an important input for the success of the new Panchayati Raj system. It should receive high priority.
- Training requirements would be a continuous process. However, it will be of a much higher intensity at the time of the introduction of new Panchayati Raj system and later on after 5 years (or before) at the time of subsequent new elections.
- Training should be provided to both officials and non-officials. In addition, orientation programmes would also be needed for MPs, MLAs, high level officials of government at state and district levels.
- Training period would be different for different categories of trainees and at different levels. The

duration of TOT programme at national level would be for two weeks. Training period for functionaries of panchayats could be three to five days plus another two days for chairpersons of PRIs at all levels. Orientation programmes could be for one to three days.

- Use of regional/local dialect to be preferred for training/orientation to people and their representatives at the village level.
- Training methodology, especially for non-official members and those at lower levels and for the public, should lay greater emphasis on audio-visual methods. This should also be reflected in TOTs and preparation of training materials.

The Workshop identified several types of training/orientation programmes and related activities. It also identified the level of training institutions suitable for each type of programme. These are given below:

Types of Training/Orientation Programmes	*Appropriate level of Training Institution*
Training of Trainers (TOT) for Master Trainers drawn from State level training institutions	National Level
National level Seminars and Workshops on specific aspects of training programme	National Level
Preparation of training material and case studies and conduct of research for the same	National Level
Orientation Programme for Members of Parliament	National Level
TOT for District and Block level training institutions/agencies	State Level*
Training/Orientation Programmes for higher level government functionaries like departmental secretaries, head of departments at the state and district levels etc.	State Level
Orientation programmes for MLAs	State Level

Types of Training/Orientation Programmes	*Appropriate level of Training Institution*
Training of Zila Parishad level elected functionaries and key officials	State Level
Training for Block level representatives and functionaries	District Level
Training for Village Panchayat level representatives and functionaries	Block Level
Awareness/Sensitivity camp at Gram Sabha level to generate the needed awareness of and familiarity with the broad provision of Constitution (Seventy-Third) Amendment Act, 1992.	Village Level

Apart from the above state levels institutions, universities including agricultural universities, were identified in general as potential institutions for training purposes. Non-Government Organisations (NGOs) were also considered as an additional resource for training of non-officials. However, it was pointed out that at the district and block levels.

- There is dearth of training institutions at the district level and more so at the block level. Hence no specific institutions were identified.
- The following functionaries could be utilised as resource persons and may be deputed for TOT programme to be conducted by the State Level Training Institutions: Deputy Development Officers, Project Officers, Assistant Project Officers, Deputy and Joint Directors of Panchayats, and Block Development Officers. The above may also include, depending upon state or district specific situations, representatives of capable NGOs, experienced ex-chairpersons of Zila Parishads.
- The work of identification of institutions at district and block level should, therefore, continue in consultation with district administration, elected heads of Panchayats at district/block levels, state advisory

committee on training and NGOs, etc.
- There may be a mobile training unit at district/block levels. The district training unit may go to blocks for imparting training.

Administrative Support

- There should be a Directorate of Training (Panchayati Raj) at the State level organising and coordinating the activities of training of officials and non-officials.
- There should be a state level advisory committee on training and other aspects of Panchayati Raj consisting of officials, and non-officials to advise the Minister in charge of Panchayats and facilitate the involvement of non-official agencies also in the training effort.
- The chairpersons of Panchayats at the district and block levels should be made responsible for coordinating training efforts at district and block levels.
- For strengthening of training infrastructure, there will be requirements for additional facilities, specialised faculty, accommodation, research, library, reading material, audio-visual aids and transportation. The union and state governments should meet these requirements.
- In view of the huge training requirements to be met in a year or two and the need for strengthening training infrastructure, it is advisable that the state governments should issue orders underlining the importance of training in the present context and releasing staff and allocating funds on a priority basis for the same.

Financial Implications

The following estimates of expenses were suggested:
- Rs.200/- per day per trainee plus actual fare, to and fro, for the trainees at state level institutions.
- Rs.150/- per trainee per day for training at district level.
- Rs.100/- per trainee per day for training at block level.
- The elected functionaries may also be paid a daily allowance of Rs.50/- per day.

- An amount of Rs.1,000/- per awareness camp at Gram Sabha level may be sanctioned for contingency expenditure on mikes, small refreshments etc.
- The training cost for TOT may be shared between the union and the state governments. The Union and the state governments should also bear the bulk of the training cost of functionaries. However, in due course, Panchayats should also bear a part of the training cost.
- Union government should provide adequate funds on a priority basis for research and studies on Panchayati Raj.

Training of Trainers Programme

The workshop suggested a module for a two-week duration for the training of trainers.

Suggested Module

- Systems Approach to Training so as to develop skills required for any training programme of this type (2 days)
- Panchayat Raj – its objectives, legal framework and the modalities of its internal functioning (3 days).
- Methodology of District/Decentralised Planning (2 ½ days).
- Programmes (1 ½ days). (Only those programmes need to be discussed which are certainly going to be with the PRIs: Poverty Alleviation, Employment Generation; and Programmes for Women and Weaker Sections).
- Team Work and Inter-departmental Coordination (1 day)
- Experience sharing – Development of Case Studies (1 day)
- Field Visit (1 day).

During 1994-95, the Ministry of Rural Development, Government of India, took the responsibility of providing TOTs in Panchayati Raj through three apex level institutions, viz. National Institute of Rural Development, National Academy of Administration, and the Indian Institute of Public

Administration. These training institutions were assigned a certain specific number of states. In these training programmes, prospective trainers were drawn from the states and in turn, they were supposed to impart training to panchayati raj functionaries, both officials and non-officials, at the state, district and sub-district levels.

Rajiv Gandhi Foundation Seminars/Workshops

The Task Force On Panchayat Raj, Rajiv Gandhi Foundation has since 1993, conducted a number of seminars/workshops regarding the working of the panchayats. Training has been one important aspect in all the deliberations of the Foundation. Some of the important recommendations are given below:

- "Training of panchayat leaders should be taken at war footing whereas an on-going training programme need to be strengthened and streamlined at state-level.
- Training should be all encompassing, covering not only statutory provisions regarding rights and respon{ibilities given in respective state Panchayat Acts but also on the concept of self-governance, inter-panchayat relations as well as the position of Gram Sabha, decentralised planning, budgetings and accounts.
- Issues related to education, drinking water, health and poverty-alleviation programmes such as Jawahar Rozgar Yojana (JRY), Employment Assurance Scheme (EAS), Integrated Rural Development Programme (IRDP), etc., should be incorporated in the contents of the training programmes. Special efforts should be made to expose the trainees to the methods of resource and social-need mapping so that PRIs could prepare their own data-bank which, in turn, will facilitate decentralised planning.
- Use of charts, graphs, slides, role plays and songs, should be made along with lectures on topics given above. Case studies, field visits as well as demonstrations should also be organised as part of training programmes. Pamphlets and other reading material in regional languages should be prepared and distributed.

- Organising orientation camps jointly for officials and panchayat leaders are crucial. Therefore, it should be done on priority basis.
- ...emphasis should be laid on the Training of Trainers (TOTs) who, in turn, would impart training in their respective areas. While selecting Master Trainers, their aptitude and inclination must be taken into consideration. Otherwise, time and resources spent on them would go in vain.
- It should be recognised that training is not a one-time exercise. It requires follow-up programmes including short reorientation/refresher courses for those who have already undergone training exercise. Therefore, a detailed documentation of training should be made at the level of district headquarters in coordination with the Directorate of Panchayats in each state.
- For the purpose of training, attempts should be made to forge operational linkages between PRIs and NGOs. The NGOs should be recognized as the fourth tool to PRIs."[27]

Initiatives by the Union Ministry of Rural Development

During 1993-94, the Ministry of Rural Development also constituted a task force on preparation of guidelines for distant education in collaboration with Indira Gandhi National Open University to develop self instructional written material as well as audio and video programmes to disseminate information regarding various aspects of panchayat raj.

The Ministry of Rural Development, Government of India, continued to provide financial assistance for strengthening/ establishment of State Institutes for Rural Development which was initiated during the Sixth Plan. Similar facility was extended for Extension Training Centres, both for strengthening and modernisation as well as for the establishment of new extension centres. Under the Extension Training Centres, Government of India, in 1993-94, provided financial assistance of Rs. 16.60 lakh for establishment of a new centre and Rs. 5.00

lakh towards non-recurring expenditure in strengthening and improvement of an existing centre.

In order to provide training to the panchayati raj functionaries, the funding pattern was modified by the Government of India during 1996-97. Up to 75 per cent of the funds allocated annually were to be utilised to intensify training related activities in selected States with particular emphasis on those who would require training for Panchayati Raj. The central assistance for this purpose was 100 per cent. Special emphasis was laid on placing core faculty in the SIRDs. The remaining funds allocated annually under the scheme were utilised to support the SIRDs.[28] The central outlay for the training during the Eighth Five Year Plan was Rs. 8.80 crore. During the Ninth Five Year Plan, the Ministry of Rural Development emphasised the need to the States to work out systematic and comprehensive training programmes for the PRIs functionaries so as to generate awareness among the masses at the grassroots level and to strengthen the Gram Sabha. Besides, the Ministry extended financial assistance to the states in their effort to train and create awareness among the PRI elected members and functionaries. The financial assistance by Government of India to the SIRDs was 100 per cent for non-recurring expenditure and 50 per cent for recurring expenditure. The scheme was, however, demand driven in nature. Special emphasis was placed on the recruitment of core faculty members in the SIRDs. Hundred per cent funding support from the Centre was available to cover expenditure on procuring the services of five core faculty members for each SIRD."[29] Keeping in view the need of the modernisation and skill development, it was decided to extend National Informatics Centre Network (NICNET) connectivity to all the SIRDs to improve their functioning. NICNET connectivity was provided to 14 SIRDs and to NIRD, Hyderabad, North East Regional Centre (NERC), NIRD, Guwahati and Council for Advancement of People's Action and Rural Technology (CAPART), New Delhi. Four SIRDs, NIRD, Hyderabad and NERC, NIRD, Guwahati were provided with multimedia equipment."[30] The Plan outlay for the year 1999-2000 for this scheme was Rs. 4.25 crore. For the Extension Training Centre (ETC), the Central assistance was 100 per cent for non-recurring expenditure and the recurring expenditure was provided for the maximum ceiling of Rs. 5 lakh per annum per ETC. The Plan Outlay of this scheme for the year 1999-2000 was Rs. 3 crore."[31] Tables 5 and 6 provide detailed break-up of funds earmarked for training of panchayati raj elected members from 1992 to 1997 and 1997-2002. Table 5 provides year-wise detailed account of the funds given to various training institutions or state governments for the purpose of training of panchayati raj elected representatives. The purpose has been not only training, but sometimes also for the preparation of training literature, etc. From 1997 to 2002 (Table 6), most of the financial assistance had gone to NGOs/institutions again for the training of panchayati raj members. As a matter of fact, from 1992 to 2002 for a period of almost ten years, approximately Rs. 21.93 crore have been spent directly in the training of panchayati raj representatives both through NGOs as well as through training institutions.

Initiatives by the Union Ministry of Panchayati Raj

An important development in the panchayati raj pertains to the establishment of a separate Ministry of Panchayati Raj on 27th May, 2004. During the year 2005-2006, Ministry of Panchayati Raj allocated Rs. 24.40 crore for training purposes. This scheme was operated on a 75:25 sharing basis with the states. It provided assistance to State institutions and NGOs etc. for providing training to the elected representatives and officials of the PRIs. It is evident that the funds from the Government of India for training of selected panchayati raj representatives were basically given to the state institutions and NGOs for imparting training to these people. Since 1992 up to 2006, approximately Rs. 46.33 crore have been allocated for this purpose.

Another important development in the training of panchayati raj elected representatives and officials relate to the Seventh Round Table of the Ministers in-charge of Panchayati Raj at Jaipur during December 17-19, 2004 regarding bringing improvement in the training programmes. The Round Table prepared a National Capability Building Framework to improve the range and content of training programmes.

The emphasis in this Round Table was to bring out a national perspective on the training and capacity building for all PRI functionaries. Some of the important elements of this Framework relate to the following aspects:

- Special effort should be made towards sensitizing the media, political parties, representatives in the legislatures, civil society organizations and citizens.
- Special campaigns for mobilization of Gram Sabha members.
- Special training for women, Scheduled Castes/ Scheduled Tribes representatives.
- Training for tribal areas should be designed so as to have regard to the cultural traditions and special needs of tribal people.
- Training and communication should be viewed as a continuous process
- Functional literacy training courses should be undertaken for those panchayat members who need it.
- Representation of panchayat members in the governing boards of training institutions.
- In the training programmes, emphasis should be given to the following subjects gender equity and social justice; human development; poverty alleviation; participatory planning, implementation and monitoring; right to information and transparency; social audit; panchayati raj rules and regulations.
- Training strategy should be participative and interactive and should also include exposure visits, satellite training, newsletters, updates etc.
- Trained members should be encouraged to become resource persons.
- To create a panchayat capacity building fund through the Ministry of Panchayati Raj, which could include a certain percentage of central transfers specially earmarked for that purpose. Similarly, state

governments should also create a panchayat capacity building fund for training.

- There should be a national perspective plan on training and capacity building for all PRI functionaries.

This document also provided the details of resource persons for implementing the framework. This consists of master resource persons, resource persons at the district level, etc. This document also provides very many aspects of the development of training materials as well; as costs of implementing the framework.

However, it was felt and as emphasized in the Annual Report of the Ministry of Panchayati Raj, Government of India for the year 2005-2006 that this framework is not adequate to meet the challenges of training and capacity building requirements of the PRIs. The Ministry is now working on a training strategy so as to bring a shift in the approach for capacity building. The Ministry proposes to provide training on priority basis to weaker sections and women representatives. The main purpose of training is to provide in the elected representatives awareness, capability to ensure accountability and fiscal prudence and attitudinal change. This approach also tries to link every gram panchayat to one extension training centre. It also proposes to make necessary changes both in terms of strengthening and upgrading extension training centre. Besides, the subjects in training would include issues on – gender, transparency, accountability, right to information act, national rural employment guarantee act, as well as problems related to agriculture, health, education, public distribution system etc.

Initiatives by other Organisations

In the training of panchayati raj functionaries, a number of other organisations also got involved. The National Commission for Women have been involved in the training of women members of panchayats. It was felt by the Commission that reservation of 1/3rd seats for women is a step towards political empowerment of nearly one million elected women panchayat members. In order to enable them to decisively participate in the developmental work, training is a very big factor. The Commission felt that of the handicaps faced by the women panchayat members relate to their ignorance regarding information and knowledge about the panchayat raj as well as the developmental schemes and programmes, etc. The training of members is an essential ingredient for mitigation of their difficulties. With this background, the Commission sponsored with the help of local NGOs a number of training camps in some parts of the country. Since 1996 the Commission also sponsored workshops/seminars to deliberate on the related issues. Some of the important recommendations that emerged are:

- All elected women members of PRIs need training for their work.
- For this purpose, as a first step, trainers would have to be trained at all levels.
- Training must deal with informational skills and related attitudinal aspects.
- The contents and curriculum may include: understanding the rules, regulations, procedures and powers of the different levels of PRIs, details of the developmental schemes PRIs are expected to implement, and the role of different Government departments and the potential to make them deliver; developing personal skills relating to self-esteem and the ability to articulate, skills for participation in a meeting, including minuting and moderating a meeting, basics of book keeping and auditing resource mobilisation and resource based local planning, collective action and popular mobilisation, networking with supportive elements in the Government and NGOs; and internalising the values of gender equity, learning to identify the gender dimensions of any scheme or project undertaken as well as schemes and projects that would promote gender equity, and the concepts of transparency and accountability.
- Training should be continuous, participative and interactive and trainers drawn from Government and NGOs.

- Training manuals/modules should be developed in English, Hindi and state languages.[32]

Panchayat Raj Training in the States

A detailed analysis was made earlier describing and analysing the training of panchayati raj representatives since the first generation of panchayati raj came into existence. The training of panchayati raj elected representatives with the financial assistance from the Government of India was given a lot of prominence in this phase. After the decline in the late sixties of the community development programme and the fact that in some states the panchayat elections were not conducted at regular intervals, a number of training institutions became dysfunctional. When one looks into the various reports of the state governments on panchayati raj in the seventies, one factor which comes out very prominently deals with the fact that training has been a neglected factor in the panchayati raj system. In most of the states, it has been observed that there has been lack of a policy on training and no systematic and sustained effort was made for the training of panchayati raj representatives. There has been ad-holism in the training programmes. The real nature of the problems in most of the states as observed by the Asoka Mehta Committee: "Training institutions have, by and large, been functioning in a low key manner in most of the States and leave much to be desired. This is attributed to constraints of resources, unsatisfactory staffing pattern, absence of a linkage with the Universities/ colleges, lack of proper physical facilities, defects in syllabus and training methodology, etc. Suitable remedial measures should be initiated with a view to resuscitate and revitalise these institutions."[33]

West Bengal

However, as far as the training of elected Panchayati Raj representatives is concerned, West Bengal has been an exception. In West Bengal, right from 1978, a well thought out scheme of training for panchayat raj representatives have been going on. It is also true that in West Bengal the panchayats were used in a powerful manner for bringing about resurgence in the rural areas. It has been rightly pointed out in this connection: "In the decade-and-a-half of their existence, the panchayats have achieved much that is tangible, especially in land reform but also in rural development generally. More than this, they have brought about a churning of the submerged humanity in the rural areas and created a high degree of social and political awareness among all sections. Thousands have entered the political process as contestants for elective posts. Those elected have had undreamt of opportunities to develop into leaders. Even at the Gram Panchayat level, Pradhans and members spoke with confidence and knowledge, not only on matters of immediate interest but on a variety of conceptual issues. These are highly encouraging developments, indicating that the panchayats have helped in strengthening the roots of democracy."[34]

The training system has been vibrant right from 1978 and subsequently it has been consolidated and stabilised in terms of syllabus for training as well as training institutions engaged in this task, funding pattern, TOTs, identification of trainers, etc.[35] Since 1992, the Government of West Bengal formulated an operating plan for the training. For this purpose, two workshops were held in 1993. Three important recommendations which were made in these workshops were: identification of resource persons/trainers; training of trainers, and creation of infrastructure in holding the training centres in a decentralised manner all over the state.

It was calculated that as the number of trainees involved was 70,000, in the first phase, the government decided to decentralise the training programme to different districts. A district level committee consisting of Chairman, Zila Parishad, (Chairman of the Committee), District Magistrate and District Panchayat Officers (as members), was established. This district level committee's primary role was to identify the resource persons as well as training centres for conducting training in the district. For this purpose, the district level committee interacted with government officials, panchayat functionaries, NGOs and academicians. Resource persons as well as the institutions to be utilised for the training were also identified. The resource persons/trainers were drawn mostly from government officials, experienced panchayat functionaries, school and college teachers, medical officers and from NGOs (actively involved in rural development and social welfare programmes). The committee identified, panchayat samiti meeting halls, cooperative training institutes, teachers training institutes, training centres of NGOs and other places as the institutions for the training of elected panchayati raj members. In all, 109 training institutions and 502 resource persons from 16 districts were identified by the district level committees. On an average, two institutions in each sub-division were chosen and five resource persons for each such institutions selected to undertake the project. Afterwards training of trainers commenced in batches of 30 members at State Institute of Panchayat (SIP) and State Institute of Rural Development (SIRD) in October, 1993. It was later on extended to other districts of the state also. Each programme comprised of lectures and discussions over a period of 5 days. The programme was residential. Besides the lectures, emphasis was also given on audio-visual aids. Intensive training was given at SIP and SIRD to the trainers for conducting courses at the district level.[36]

Training Curriculum: The training curriculum was developed in the following five modules:

- Role of panchayats as a unit of Local Self-Government;
- Problems and issues related to people below the poverty line, illiteracy, gender bias, unemployment and under-employment, health and sanitation, population and pollution with the objective of sensitising the opinion leaders of the panchayats on the issues;
- Poverty alleviation programmes and the role of panchayats in planning and implementation of the activities;
- Development and people's participation;
- Planning for villages/block/district comprising objective setting, preparation of resource inventory, identification of problem areas, determining strategy, and integration of existing development programmes.[37]

Initially, the emphasis of training was at the gram panchayat level only. However, during the year 1993-94, the Government of West Bengal, (out of the funds available from the state government, United Nations International Childrens Educational Fund (UNICEF) and Government of India) allotted to 16 districts according to their requirements on a scale of Rs. 6,900 for each training course of 18 hours for 40 participants on an average. The expenditure comprised of messing charges of participants, resource persons and supporting persons Rs. 30/- per head per day for 3 days, honorarium of Rs. 50/- per lecture hour for 18 such hours and the rest for contingencies charges. It was calculated that the total requirement of fund for the current phase of training of about 70,000 members would be to the tune of Rs. 12 million.[38]

Madhya Pradesh

It is now proposed to provide an over-view of the Panchayati Raj Training in Madhya Pradesh since 1993. The training was initiated from the financial support of UNICEF. The training was provided by the NGOs in a 3-day course of training based on the manuals, prepared by the Department of Rural Development, Government of Madhya Pradesh, Bhopal. The status of panchayati raj training as on October, 1997 is given below:

Panchayat Raj Institutions	*Participants*	*Total No. of Persons*	*No. of Persons Trained*	*No. of Persons yet to be Trained*
Zila Parishad	Adhyakshes	45	42	3
Zila Parishad	Upadhyakshes	45	43	2
Zila Parishad	Members	856	856	..
Janpad Panchayat	Adhyakshes	459	459	..
Janpad Panchayat	Upadhyakshes	459	459	..
Janpad Panchayat	Members	9097	9097	..
Gram Panchayat	Sarpanches	30922	30922	..
Gram Panchayat	Panches	443429	30922	412507

Source: Sharan, S.V. 1998. Panchayati Raj Training in Madhya Pradesh: An Evaluation. New Delhi: Institute of Social Sciences. p.1.

Training Through Satellite:

Zila Parishad	Members	541
Janpad Panchayat	Adhyakshes	55
Janpad Panchayat	Upadhyakshes	214
Janpad Panchayat	Members	4131
Total		4921

Source: Sharan, S.V. 1998. Panchayati Raj Training in Madhya Pradesh: An Evaluation. New Delhi: Institute of Social Sciences. P.1.

It is evident from the above table that the elected functionaries of the Zila and Janpad Panchayats were trained. However, the bulk of panches about 4.12 lakh were not given any training. Most of the training was conducted by the Academy of Administration, Bhopal, State Institute of Rural Development (SIRD), Jabalpur and National Institute for Rural Development (NIRD), Hyderabad as well as 12 government training institutions and 34 centres in selected NGOs. These 34 UNICEF supported NGOs provided training for sarpanches, upsarpanches, women panches, and sachivs from gram panchayats. This training was centred in 68 blocks of 40 districts in 1995. These NGOs trained over 23,000 persons by organising 3-day training courses on the basis of the manuals prepared by the Department of Rural Development, Government of Madhya Pradesh. Similarly, 20 NGOs worked in 31 districts during 1996. Approximately 37,423 persons were trained by UNICEF supported NGOs from 1995 to June 1997.

During 1994-95, the Academy of Administration, Bhopal trained 42 chairmen and 43 vice-chairmen of zila panchayats, 413 chairmen of janpad panchayats, 235 master trainers, 21 janpad members, 38 sarpanches, etc. Some chairpersons of standing committees were also trained during 1997. Besides, the Academy of Administration also produced reading materials on: panchayat sachivs/karmis; sarpanches; janpad members; literature on administrative control; leadership, employment skills, etc.

The SIRD at Jabalpur trained functionaries like chairmen and vice-chairmen, janpad, chairpersons of standing committees, sarpanches, master trainers, etc. In this training, 5-day course was provided for janpad, chairmen and vice-chairmen and 3-day course for sarpanches. The subjects covered for training of vice-chairmen, janpad were: coordination; beneficiaries under development schemes; schemes for women and children; issues relating to SCs/STs; and education, health, planning, etc.

Similarly, the other training centres/institutes in the area of rural development also trained the master trainers and sarpanches. During 1996-97, 10 regional rural development centres together trained 85 sarpanches, 384 master trainers, besides training officers at the block level. Training of panchayati raj functionaries like: chairpersons, vice-chairpersons of Zila Parishad and chairpersons of standing committees of zila parishad was conducted at NIRD, Hyderabad.

Efforts were also made to provide training through satellite and 4921 functionaries received training through this method. The content of training through satellite was limited to health, education, drinking water, development of women and children, employment oriented schemes: JRY, EAS, IRDP and some provisions of the Constitution (Seventy-third) Amendment Act and the Madhya Pradesh Panchayat Act. Some of the important aspects of panchayati raj like concept of self-governance, position of the Gram Sabha in the panchayat system, mandatory and other functions of the gram panchayat, inter-panchayat relations, panchayat relations with government, planning, budget, accounts and audit, revenue matters, procedural aspects were not covered.

Master trainers in this campaign of training were drawn from different sources – government service, academic institutions, training institutions, NGOs, etc. These trainers trained sarpanches, upsarpanches, panches and some Gram Sabha members. It has been pointed out that in the selection of these master trainers their attitude and ability for imparting training was not kept in view. As a result, many of the master trainers lacked interest and were indifferent to the programme. It has also been pointed out that in these training programmes, the following problems were identified:

1. duration of training was short
2. poor attendance

3. content of training was inadequate
4. methodology of training was generally lecture based
5. training institutes/centres were not well equipped
6. trainers lacked motivation

Besides, no allocation was given for organising refresher courses for those who were already trained and also no steps were taken to train around 4.12 lakh panches and others who had not been trained at all. It was also mentioned that there was a need to develop training strategy to take care of short term and long term requirements: "categories of persons to be trained; frequency and duration of training; its contents and methodology; quality of trainers; availability of infrastructure and financial support; monitoring and evaluation are some of the core elements which should go into the designing of the training programme."[39]

Two factors relating to state training institutes and regional rural development training centres also need to be elaborated. One factor deals with the fact that around 68 per cent of the posts of instructors in these institutions have been lying vacant. Secondly, there is no library worth the name at any institute/centre. It has also been pointed out that the attendance at the training courses was quite poor. For the training organised by the SIRD, Jabalpur and various regional rural development centres, the attendance varied from 3 to 19 per course. Some of the important observations regarding the training of panchayati raj representatives during 1995-97 are: range of subjects covered in the training programmes were limited; training syllabus was fixed while the background and needs of trainees were varied; training aids were not adequately used; training period was short; training institutes/centres were in a bad shape; infrastructural support for training at the training institutes/centres or for the training teams was far too inadequate; many of the trainers were indifferent and lacked motivation; satellite training was not effective; there was no follow-up or an impact study; social profile of elected functionaries was not available; there was no monitoring of the training programme; and there was lack of coordination among training agencies and between the training agencies and the government.

During 1997-98, for panchayati raj training the Annual Report of the Department of Panchayati and Rural Development, Government of Madhya Pradesh, has mentioned the following details of the programmes which were conducted by SIRD, Jabalpur:

Training programmes	*Number of training programmes*	*Number of participant who attended*
1997-98		
Chairman, Janpad Panchayat	3	8
Vice-Chairman, Janpad Panchayat	9	32
Chairman of Subject Committees Of Janpad Panchayat	23	202
Master Trainers	5	52
2000-2001		
Chairman/Vice-Chairman, Janpad Panchayat	22	480

Source: Administrative Report, Government of Madhya Pradesh, Department of Rural Development, 1997-98, p.17 and year 2000-2001, p. 22.

On 24th May, 2000, the Government of Madhya Pradesh took the following policy decision regarding the training of panchayati raj representatives.

- The elected representatives of zila panchayat (district panchayat) and janpad panchayat (intermediate panchayat) should be trained in institutions which have been identified for this purpose.
- Those representatives who could not attend these programmes should be requested to join the programme for the next financial year.
- For the purpose of training of elected representatives of gram panchayats, a coordination committee at the district level should be constituted consisting of the following:

Chairman, Zila Panchayat	Chairperson
District Collector	Member
Chief Executive Officer of Zila Panchayat	Member

The above committee will select the NGOs for the purpose of training of gram panchayat representatives. The district coordination committee will select the trainers on the following basis: educational qualifications; previous experience; and general personality.

- The trainers who were selected earlier will be again evaluated about their suitability for this work.
- The training manual will be published by the state government and it will be used for the purpose of training at SIRD, Jabalpur.

Appraisal of the Training Programmes (1976–2006)

A major shift in the panchayati raj training of rural development officials as well as elected panchayati raj representatives took place with the transfer of training institutions which were earlier managed and controlled by the Ministry of Community Development, Cooperation and Panchayati Raj, Government of India, to the state governments. In fact, with the decline of community development, there was also a perceptible decline in training activities from 1969 to 1992. More so, for non-officials of panchayati raj as the PRIs entered a phase of decline due to variety of reasons. As such, the centralised system of training in the broad area of rural development and panchayati raj came to an end. However, another important factor which need to be emphasised relates to the fact that since the early 70s, there was a lot of emphasis on poverty alleviation and direct attacks on poverty and this policy of the Government of India got strengthened in the Sixth Five Year Plan. Even before this, the Ministry of Rural Development, Government of India, again assumed a direct responsibility in 1974-75 under the Drought Prone Areas Programme (DPAP) and, since then, a large number of programmes pertaining to DPAP were organized by the Ministry of Rural Development, Government of India.

Gradually, training courses concerned with the other subject like Integrated Rural Development Programme (IRDP) and Training of Rural Youth in Self-Employment (TRYSEM) were included on a regular basis and there was an increase in the tempo year by year from 1974-75 in poverty related programmes mainly for the officials. The Government of India identified a number of functionaries including central government functionaries at the senior level as well as state government officers from areas dealing with the rural development (both at the senior, middle and district level) were also drawn in the training. There was also a mention in these programmes of non-officials like MPs, MLAs, MLCs, Chairmen of Zila Parishads and their standing committees, Chairmen of Panchayat Samities and their standing committees, sarpanches, etc.

From 1981-82, emphasis was also given besides sectoral training programmes to national conferences, national seminars/workshops and regional seminars/workshops pertaining to mostly poverty related issues. The Ministry of Rural Development also established a training division for organising the training programmes. Almost all the training institutions in the country both national and state level, were drawn in this effort. A cursory look at the Annual Reports of Ministry of Rural Development from 1974-75 to 1992-93 reveals that there was a tremendous surge in training activities relating to poverty alleviation programmes and geared towards training of officials in a large number of areas of concern. There was a decline in the training of panchayati raj representatives. However, since 1993, some thinking had started in the area of training of elected panchayati raj representatives. From 1969 to 1993, i.e. almost 25 years, there was a dilution in the training of panchayati raj representatives. The efforts which have been made since the commencement of (Seventy-third) Amendment Act primarily relate to those made by National Institute of Rural Development (NIRD), the Indian Institute of Public Administration (IIPA) and a number of seminars by Rajiv Gandhi Foundation on various aspects of panchayati raj. During the 8th, 9th and 10th Plans, emphasis was on strengthening of SIRDs and ETCs in various states for imparting training to the elected representatives. Besides, funds were also given to the NGOs for conducting training programmes. However, these programmes did not touch in a significant manner the elected representatives at the village panchayat and intermediate panchyat levels. Almost in all the states, except in West Bengal, some kind of training was given to the elected representatives at the district panchayat level alone. As such, there is lack of coherent training policy for members of the PRIs. The magnitude of the task is very large as about 30 lakh representatives have to be trained and most of these representatives are first timers. This fact has also to be seen in the context of the fact that 1/3rd women have come in the mainstream of panchayati raj and there is considerable number of persons belonging to the Scheduled Castes/Scheduled Tribes in these institutions.

In this connection, another point which needs emphasis is that a number of other agencies are also engaged in the training of panchayati raj leaders. This includes National Commission for Women and CAPART which is helping NGOs to organise training programmes and provides financial assistance for the same. This analysis gives an overview of the activities conducted since the last 14 years in this area. There is ad-hocism. The emphasis is on strengthening the training infrastructure at the state and district levels. There is no coherent policy on training regarding the training programmes, the coverage, the methodology, syllabus, etc.

However, since 1978, West Bengal has done a remarkable work in this area. This state has a well coordinated plan for training of panchayati raj representatives, the whole system is decentralised, the resource persons are drawn from academics, NGOs, government functionaries and the curriculum is also well devised, the coverage is also very large and there is a proper funding to the various districts. In Madhya Pradesh, the training programmes for the elected panchayati raj representatives were conducted through UNICEF grant. These programmes were conducted in some of the districts of the state taking the help of the rural development training infrastructure on the one side and the NGOs on the other. A number of limitations have been observed in these programmes: short duration of training, poor attendance, content of training inadequate, methodology was defective and trainers lacked motivation and some important aspects of panchayati raj were not touched at all. Representatives at the village panchayat level have not been able to get any training at all.

REFERENCES

1. Quoted in Editorial. 1961. Training for Community Development. *Kurukshetra,* 9(9). June. 1961. p. 2.
2. India. Committee on Plan Projects. 1957. *Report of the Team For The Study of Community Projects And National Extension Service, Vol. 1.* New Delhi. (Chairman: Balvantray Mehta). p. 7.
3. Rao, G.V.K. 1961. Training for Community Development: A Bird's Eye-View. *Kurukshetra,* 9(9). June. P. 37.
4. India. Ministry of Community Development and Co-Operation, Department of Community Development. *Annual Report* 1962-63. New Delhi. p. 24.
5. India. Ministry of Community Development and Cooperation, Department of Community Development. 1960. *From Lok Sabha to Gram Sabha.* New Delhi. p.20.
6. Ibid. p. 4.
7. India. Ministry of Community Development and Co-Operation, Department of Community Development. *Report 1959-60.* New Delhi. p. 21.
8. India. Ministry of Community Development and Co-operation, Department of Community Development. *Report 1961-62.* p. 25.
9. Ibid. p. 27.
10. Ibid. p. 61.
11. Ibid. pp. 26-27.
12. India. Ministry of Community Development and Cooperation, Department of Community Development. *Annual Report 1964-65.* New Delhi. p. 42.
13. India. Ministry of Community Development and Cooperation, Department of Community Development. *Annual Conference of Community Development and Panchayati Raj, 20 July to 22 July,* 1964. Agenda & Notes. New Delhi. pp. 148-150. (Mimeo)
14. India. Ministry of Community Development and Co-operation, Department of Community Development. 1959. *Report of A Community Development Evaluation Mission In India.* New Delhi. p. 83.

15. Jain, S. C. 1967. *Community Development and Panchayati Raj in India*. New Delhi: Allied. pp. 510-511.
16. Malkani, N. R. 1961. Training of Non-Officials. *Kurukshetra*, 9(9). June. p. 11.
17. Jain, S. C. *op. cit.* p. 509.
18. Malkani, N. R. *op. cit.* p. 11.
19. Jain, S. C. *op. cit.* p. 504.
20. Malkani, N. R. *op. cit.* p.11.
21. Mukherji, B. 1961. Problems of Training. *Kurukshetra*, 9(9). June. p. 8.
22. Malkani, N. R. *op. cit.* p. 10.
23. Jain, S. C. *op. cit.* pp. 511-512.
24. Rao, P.V. Narasimha. 1993. Democratic discipline – must for success of Constitution (73rd Amendment) Act, 1992. *Kurukshetra*. September. p.25.
25. Text of the recommendations of the Conference of the Ministers and Secretaries in-charge of Panchayats of States and Union Territories on the Constitution (73rd Amendment) Act, 1992. New Delhi. 3rd July, 1993. *Kurukshetra*. September, 1993. p.28.
26. *Workshop on Strategy for Training Under New Panchayati Raj:* A Report, 30th July, 1993. New Delhi. IIPA. p.1. (Mimeo).
27. Dialogue on Panchayat. 1999. Task Force on Panchayati Raj: Rajiv Gandhi Foundation. New Delhi. pp. 20-21.
28. India. Ministry of Rural Development, Department of Rural Development. *Annual Report* 1993-94. New Delhi. p. 73., and *Annual Report* 1996-97. p. 87.
29. India. Ministry of Rural Areas and Employment. *Annual Report* 1997-98. New Delhi. p. 88., and *Annual Report* 1999-2000. p.77.
30. India. Ministry of Rural Development. *Annual Report* 1999-2000. New Delhi. p. 77.
31. Ibid. p. 78.
32. India. National Commission for Women. *Annual Report* 1996-97. New Delhi. p. 39.
33. India. Ministry of Agricultural and Irrigation, Department of Rural Development. 1978. Report of The Committee on Panchayati Raj Institutions. New Delhi. (Chairman: Asoka Mehta). pp. 139-140.
34. Mukerjee, Nirmal and D. Bandopadhyay.1992. *New Horizons for West Bengal Panchayats*. Report on the Panchayats in West Bengal. Government of West Bengal. Calcutta. pp. 216-217.
35. De Amalendu. 1982. Panchayat *Training System in Panchayats in*

West Bengal (From 1978-79 to 1980-81). A Review, Government of West Bengal. Department of Panchayats and Community Development. pp.25-37.

36. West Bengal. Directorate of Panchayats. 1994. Documentation on West Bengal Panchayat. *Systematic Training Oo Elected Panchayat Members*. Calcutta. pp.3-5.
37. Ibid. p.6.
38. Ibid. p.7.
39. Sharan, S.V. 1998. *Panchayat Raj Training in Madhya Pradesh: An Evaluation*. Institute of Social Sciences. New Delhi. pp. 1-6 and 40-41.

4

Determining Training Needs and Designing the Programmes

It is now proposed to identify the core characteristics of tasks and responsibilities of the elected panchayati raj representatives as envisaged in the (Seventy-third) Amendment Act, 1992. Article 40 of the Constitution states: "the State shall take steps to organise village panchayats and endow them with such powers and authority as may be necessary to enable them to function as units of self-government". This has been further re-enforced by introducing a new Part-IX and the Eleventh Schedule to the Constitution through the Constitution (Seventy-third) Amendment Act, 1992. The most relevant provision in Part-IX is the Article 243G, which deals with the powers, authority and responsibilities of panchayats, "Subject to the provisions of the Constitution, the Legislature of a State may, by law, endow the Panchayats with such powers and authority as may be necessary to enable them to function as institutions of self-government and such law may contain provisions for the devolution of powers and responsibilities upon the Panchayats at the appropriate level, subject to such conditions as may be specified therein, with respect to (a) the preparation of plans for economic development and social justice; and (b) the implementation of such schemes for economic development and social justice as may be entrusted to them including those in relation to the matters listed in the Eleventh Schedule."

In the context of the Article 243-G as mentioned above, the expression "Devolution" means that "when the authority in respect of a specific activity is transferred from the state to the local governments, the latter should have the prerogative of taking decisions in the matters of planning and implementation of such activity."[1] It is also important to emphasise that for effective implementation of their decisions, the panchayats also need resources and staff support. As a matter of fact, functions, funds and functionaries complement one another in matters relating to devolution of responsibilities and powers. The 29 subjects listed in the Eleventh Schedule (Table 13) could be devolved upon the panchayats.

Article 243-H vests powers in the State legislatures to:

- Authorise Panchayats to levy, collect and appropriate taxes, duties, tolls and fees.
- Assign taxes, duties, tolls and fees levied and collected by the States to Panchayats.
- Provide for making grants-in-aid to the Panchayats from the Consolidated Fund of the State; and
- Provide for constitution of Funds for crediting all money received by or on behalf of Panchayats and also the withdrawal of such money therefrom.

However, the Eleventh Finance Commission in its Report June, 2000, pointed out that in most of the states, panchayati raj bodies have not transferred schemes relating to the subjects included in the Eleventh Schedule. The Report further mentioned that, in many states, legislation relating to panchayati raj merely provided the subjects indicated in the schedule but did not specify schemes that have to be included by these bodies as prescribed in Article 243-G. As a result "funds and the functionaries relating to these schemes continue to remain under the control of the departments of the State Governments."[2] Besides, in "some cases, the implementation of some programmes has been entrusted to these bodies but only as agency function and they have no role in the planning and formulation of the schemes."[3] The Report mentioned also that functions and schemes of the panchayats should be part and parcel of the legislation which is mandatory for the states to do. However, in some states, although the legislation provides for the local bodies to levy certain taxes, but necessary rules have not been formulated or the notifications laying down the rules have not been issued. Although the state legislation contemplates a hierarchical structure of the panchayats with organic relationship within three tiers and each higher level body supervising, advising, and coordinating the activities of the lower panchayat, this role has not been categorically delineated in the State legislation and most of the time this matter has been decided by way of executive instructions. This, in turn, gives rise to the lot of uncertainty in the matter. The Report also pointed out that the Government is implementing a large number of schemes under the Centrally sponsored schemes. Most of these schemes are implemented through special agencies created at the district level. Although in some schemes the local bodies have been associated, but mostly they perform agency functions with no categorical role in the formulation and implementation of these schemes. The District Rural Development Agencies (DRDAs) are functioning as instruments of central government for planning and implementing of these schemes. The Ministry of Rural Development is the nodal ministry "to ensure that the local bodies function as institutions of self-government and all impediments to the realisation of this ideal are removed."[4] Unless this Ministry take the initiative, it may be futile to expect other Ministries in the Central Government to take action for the transfer of more schemes relating to subjects included in the schedule to the panchayats.

Similarly, "The Report of the Task Force on Devolution of Powers and Functions upon Panchayati Raj Institutions", Government of India, August, 2001[5] also pointed out that the legislation enacted by the states have not significantly altered "the functional domain of the Panchayats" and the panchayats are still performing their traditional civic functions. Consequently, in most of the states the PRIs are not very clear about the role they are expected to play in rural development. In several states, though functions are legally listed for the PRIs, but these are planned and implemented by the line departments and formal approval is taken from the Standing Committee of the district or intermediate level panchayats. As a result, there is no "role-clarity with regard to the statutory functions assigned to them." A similar situation exists in most of the states where requisite staff have not been transferred to the panchayats. Similarly, very few states have granted some element of financial autonomy to the PRIs. While the Constitution has authorised the states to transfer those 29 items of development administration, no attempt has been made to clarify as to which item would be assigned to the different tiers of the panchayats. This has been left as an executive decision to be taken by the respective states.

The Report further provided an overview of the basic issues in the devolution of functions. It also provided administrative powers and inter-tier allocation of functions as well as devolution of financial powers. On the basis of these measures, the report has analysed activity mapping among the three tiers on all the 29 subjects included in the Eleventh Schedule.[6] Besides, it also provideds the activity-wise transfer of functions and functionaries alongwith funds to each tier of panchayats.[7] The Report of the Standing Committee on Urban and Rural Development (2002) with regard to the issue of devolution observed that:

- the corresponding devolution in respect of funds and functionaries was not done
- the bureaucracy was not willing to transfer the powers to the elected representatives
- all the Department in various States dealing with the developmental activities like Irrigation, Agriculture, etc., excepting the Revenue Department, should be brought under Panchayat
- there should be an exclusive Union Ministry to look after the issues related to Panchayats.[8]

The Report of the Standing Committee pointed out the current status of the devolution of subjects in various States/Union territories in the following words: "only one State *i.e.* Karnataka has transferred funds, functions and functionaries for all the 29 subjects listed in the Eleventh Schedule. Though Kerala,

Rajasthan, Tamil Nadu, West Bengal and Daman & Diu have transferred 29 subjects to the Panchayats, they have not transferred the funds and functionaries of subjects entrusted to the Panchayats. However, in several States/Union territories, the position of the subjects transferred to Panchayats *vis-à-vis* funds, functions and functionaries is nil."[9]

The Report of the Task Force on Devolution of Powers & Functions Upon Panchayati Raj Institutions 2001 recommended that major administrative and financial powers to the PRIs may be devolved keeping in view the following principles:

- "It should facilitate preparation of plans and implementation of schemes for economic development and social justice;
- The State Government can exercise its discretion to entrust any scheme of economic and social development in addition to those covered under the 29 subjects given in the Eleventh Schedule;
- It should enable the Panchayats to function as institutions of self-government ; and
- What is appropriate at a given tier of the Panchayat should be done at that tier and not at a higher tier."[10]

On the basis of the above principles, the Report of the Task Force devolved the following powers (executive and financial) on the panchayats.[11]

Core Characteristics of Tasks and Responsibilities

District Panchayat (DP)

- To prepare, finalise and execute schemes and activities relating to subjects devolved on the District Panchayat and schemes assigned by the Central and State Governments.
- To prepare District Panchayat level plan containing the plans of different Intermediate Panchayats and Village Panchayats.
- To coordinate and oversee the functioning of any other agency which may be existing or established for development and social justice measures in consonance

with the statutory provisions and role of the District Panchayat.

- To promote capacity building measures for elected representatives and the staff working in or associated with the Panchayati Raj Institutions.
- To ensure regular and comprehensive maintenance and auditing of accounts of the District Panchayat.
- To impose taxes, cesses, levies, etc. levy user charges and develop endowments for income generation, as permissible.
- To prepare and finalise annual budget estimates of the District Panchayat.
- To constitute a District Panchayat Fund and operate it for authorised purposes.
- To sanction loans, contingent expenses, etc., for authorised purposes.
- To borrow money from banks, financial institutions, etc., for authorised purposes.
- To inspect utilisation of funds in respect of various schemes under implementation within its jurisdiction.
- To acquire, lease, and/or to transfer property.

Intermediate Panchayat (IP)

- To prepare and implement schemes of economic development and social justice as well as oversee the implementation of schemes by the other agencies within its jurisdiction.
- To prepare Plans for the Intermediate Panchayat, taking into account plans of Village panchayats.
- To cooperate in the monitoring and supervision of the execution of such works and activities as may be sponsored by the District Panchayat within its area.
- To implement/supervise any work as entrusted to it by the District Panchayat or any other higher level body.
- To maintain assets, properties, etc., of the Intermediate Panchayat.
- To impose tax and collect cesses, levies, etc., levy user

charges and develop endowments for income generation.

- To prepare and finalise its annual budget estimates.
- To constitute the Intermediate Panchayat Fund and operate it for authorised purposes.
- To inspect utilisation of funds of different schemes under implementation.
- To acquire, lease, and/or to transfer property.

Village Panchayat (VP)

- To identify and prioritise developmental schemes within its jurisdiction.
- To identify beneficiaries of poverty alleviation/ beneficiary oriented programmes.
- To decide location of projects of local relevance.
- To supervise the implementation of schemes for economic development and social justice and such other activities as may be taken up at the local initiative or assigned by the Intermediate Panchayat or District Panchayat.
- To cooperate with the Intermediate Panchayat as regards appropriate works and development schemes with regard to programmes to be taken by Intermediate Panchayats.
- To maintain the assets, properties, etc., of the Village Panchayat.
- To prepare Action Plans for Poverty Alleviation Programmes.
- To impose taxes, levy user charges and develop endowments for income generation.
- To prepare and finalise its annual budget estimates.
- To constitute a Village Panchayat Fund and operate it for authorised purposes.
- To borrow money from banks, financial institutions, etc., for authorized purposes.
- Full financial powers for payment of salaries to all the staff working under the Panchayats, even though the funds may come from the Government.

The Committee System

It is a well known fact that PRIs function through a well structured system of subject committees. The powers of these committees are defined in the respective Panchayati Raj Act of the states. Practically all the elected members have to become members of different standing committees. This provides the members an opportunity to participate in the decision-making and implementation processes. These committees also provide a forum whereby the official machinery on the one hand and the non-official structure on the other has been built in a systematic manner. Through these committees, the powers for administrative sanctions to works and schemes, acceptance of tenders and contracts, etc., are distributed to the Chief Executive Officer, the Chairman of Subjects Committees, and the District Panchayat in an ascending order. The powers of these subject committees as such relate to control of works and schemes in their charge, ensuring preparation and sanction of estimates of works and developmental schemes and supervising their execution. These are some of the obligatory powers of the subject committees. The non-obligatory powers relate to inspection of immovable property, development works and schemes, calling for information, returns, statements from Chairman or any officer or servant of the district panchayat, taking a periodical review of the progress of activities of the district panchayat. As such, the committee system provides and promotes a decentralised pattern of democracy and also decentralised administration and prevents concentration of powers in a single individual. The president of district panchayat and chief executive officer play an important role in bringing about the necessary coordination between different committees and different department of the district panchayat. All these built-in arrangements promote the necessary amount of coordination between the standing committees and various departments of the district panchayat.

The committee system has an important bearing on the powers and functions of officer bearers of the PRIs. The powers and functions of the office bearers at each level of Panchayati raj have been provided in the statutes of panchayat raj of the states. The office bearers of district panchayat, intermediate panchayat and village panchayat and the chairmen of subject committees at all levels enjoy a wide variety of administrative and financial powers. A number of reports, which have evaluated the working of panchayati raj in different states over a period of last 40 years, have pointed out that, with a few exceptions, the performance of the office bearers has not been quite satisfactory, particularly in relation to activities like involvement of people in various types of programmes, taking initiative in starting new projects and schemes, taking steps to remove bottlenecks in the implementation of programmes, etc.

District Planning Committee

Another important feature regarding the training of elected panchayati raj representatives deals with the district planning. The provision regarding District Planning Committee (DPC) has been made vide Article 243ZD of the Constitution, inserted through the Seventy-Fourth Amendment. It is mandatory for the states to constitute the DPC in every district. The following are the provisions regarding DPC:

- There shall be constituted in every State at the district level a DPC to consolidate the plans prepared by the Panchayats and the Municipalities in the district and to prepare a draft development plan for the district as a whole.
- The Legislature of a State may, by law, make provisions with respect to: (a) the composition of the DPC; (b) the manner in which the seats in such Committees shall be filled: provided that not less than four-fifths of the total number of members of such Committee shall be elected by, and from amongst, the elected members of the Panchayat at the district level and of the Municipalities in the district in proportion to the ratio between the population of the rural areas and of the urban areas in the district; (c) the functions relating to district planning which may be assigned to such Committees; and (d) the manner in which the Chairpersons of such Committees shall be chosen.

- Every DPC shall, in preparing the draft development plan, (a) have regard to: (i) matters of common interests between the Panchayats and the Municipalities including spatial planning, sharing of water and other physical and natural resources, the integrated development of infrastructure and environmental conservation; (ii) the extent and type of available resources whether financial or otherwise; (b) consult such institutions and organisations as the Governor may, by order, specify.
- The Chairperson of every DPC shall forward the development plan, as recommended by such committee, to the Government of the State.

Many States are yet to constitute the DPCs. Only fourteen States, namely, Bihar, Chhattisgarh, Goa, Haryana, Himachal Pradesh, Karnataka, Kerala, Madhya Pradesh, Manipur, Orissa, Rajasthan, Sikkim, Tamil Nadu, West Bengal and four Union Territories, Andaman and Nicobar Islands, Daman and Diu, Dadar and Nagar Haveli and Lakshadweep have taken action to constitute DPCs. In many States, DPCs are being chaired by Ministers or officers of the State Government, which is against the spirit of the Constitution (Seventy-third) Amendment Act.[12]

It is important to emphasise that in the district planning sector most of the schemes are on-going schemes, leaving little choice with the districts both in terms of financial resources as well as physical targets. As a result, the present procedure has not yet conferred the necessary degree of autonomy regarding utilisation of funds at the district level. Most of these are departmental schemes transferred to the district plan sector, leaving no choice to the local level planners. It is proposed to provide on the basis of the spirit of the constitutional provisions regarding DPC the core characteristics of tasks and the training requirements for the members of the DPC. For the purpose of this study, we are analysing from the perspective of the functions and responsibilities assigned to the DPC.

It is also true that many of the states, while formulating their Panchayat Raj Acts, incorporated, by and large, all the 29 items mentioned above. Looking into the spirit of the (Seventy-third) Amendment Act pertaining to devolution of functions and responsibilities, an attempt has been made below to identify the core characteristics of functions at different levels keeping in mind the overall perspective of the transferred subjects. In the devolution of functions to the PRIs, it is important to emphasise that these institutions derive their authority from the state legislation. The responsibilities given to those agencies under the (Seventy-third) Amendment are mainly developmental. The whole idea is to provide responsive administration in terms of some freedom to adjust programmes according to local needs, mobilisation of local resources to increase the quantum of developmental effort and also accountability for the effective implementation of programmes. There is another aspect of this devolution in the context of planning which has to be seen from the perspective that most of the programmes assigned to these institutions are in the nature of centrally sponsored schemes with very detailed guidelines in terms of planning, finance, and the target group, etc. Consequently, the PRIs are not free to alter these allocations. As such, there is a little initiative left with the PRIs in the developmental schemes. It is also true that the resources raised by these institutions at their level are limited which does not provide much scope for planning in the areas of concern with freedom. Looking from this point of view, it becomes obvious that the PRIs, in the present context, are like agencies of the state government rather than units of local government. Another aspect which need to be highlighted while detailing the training requirements at different levels is the fact that in planning the main function is being performed by the District Panchayat. There are many factors which are responsible for this. The District is the most important unit for systematic planning. Its area and population are large enough to facilitate drawing up of a viable cohesive development plan. Administrative structure and physical capabilities are available at this place. Besides, the district panchayat also plays an important advisory and supervisory role over Village panchayat and Intermediate panchayat. It also provides coordination among various intermediate panchayats and maintains close rapport with the state government. Besides, the intermediate panchayat is another important unit charged with the responsibility of planning as well as implementation of development programmes. The intermediate panchayats exercise supervision and control over the village panchayats especially with regard to the finance and implementation of various programmes. Looking from a wider perspective, it is evident that the district panchayats primarily focus on planning and coordination, while the intermediate panchayats are implementing agencies.

Perception of Elected Representatives

To understand the perception of panchayati raj representatives about their role and responsibilities as well as their views about the training imparted, a meeting was arranged at Indore (Madhya Pradesh) to elicit the views of the members of the district panchayat, intermediate panchayati and village panchayat and DPC. A cross-section of elected panchayati raj representatives were interviewed. Some of the important observations of the elected panchayati raj representatives are given below:

- At the Village Panchayat level, there is very poor understanding of the role and responsibilities as well as understanding of the various developmental programmes. This holds true at the Intermediate Panchayat level as well as District Panchayat level. Their understanding is also poor regarding the budget as well as planning.
- The members are not clear about their role and responsibilities as well as their powers vis-à-vis the officials. The representatives also categorically stated that this has not been made clear to them both in the training so far imparted to them as well as by the officials who are working in the Panchayats.
- Most of the representatives at least at the level of District Panchayat and Intermediate Panchayat had undergone some kind of training. However, it was pointed out that the training was not very relevant.

- It is difficult for the Panchayat members to leave their place of work and go to far off places for training. As a result, there is lot of absenteeism in the training programmes.
- It was suggested that there is a need to conduct training programmes at the district, block and village levels for the panchayati raj representatives at locations convient to them.
- The training should be undertaken during the lean season and there should be at least two training programmes (for each level) in a year.

Training needs Identification

Methodology

The methodology adopted for the purpose of identification of training needs of the panchayati raj representatives is based on the analysis of core characteristics of functions/tasks in each category, i.e. district panchayat, intermediate panchayat and village panchayat and Gram Sabha. Besides, emphasis has also been given to tasks and functions performed by the president, vice-president and members of standing committees at all levels. Identification of the training needs has also been carried out in case of members and office bearers of the district planning committee. In all these categories, looking at the various functions in each category, training objectives have been identified both in terms of essential and desirable aspects.

District Panchayat

Category: Members of District Panchayat

Core Characteristics of Tasks	Training Objectives
Understanding and awareness about local self-government. Preparation of plans and implementation of schemes for economic development	*Essential* Democratic decentralisation, history of Panchayati Raj in India, salient characteristics of the Seventy-third Amendment Act and salient characteristics of the concerned State

and social justice Coordination and consolidation of the plans of Intermediate Panchayats	Government Act. Knowledge of multi-level planning Knowledge of decentralised planning: preparation of plans, identification of resources and data base. Familiarity with objectives, contents and methodology of the District Plan. Awareness of development linkages to integrate the plans of the Intermediate Panchayats: i. Inter-sectoral or horizontal linkages; and ii. Linkages between various levels of administrative hierarchy or vertical linkages ***Desirable*** Familiarity with the process of planning at the national and state levels. Familiarity with the concept of spatial planning.
To ensure the implementa-tion of schemes and programmes of central, and state governments and schemes undertaken from own resources and oversee-ing their implementation on the basis of guidelines and other necessary require-ments.	***Essential*** Knowledge of broad objectives, strategy, targets, etc. of development programmes. A thorough understanding of the modalities of various development programmes, eligibility for assistance under these programmes, pattern of financial assistance in respect of specific schemes, administration of subsidy, requirements of institutional credit, knowledge of the lending rates for loans, and terms finances available for various schemes, etc.

	Understanding of the implementation process of plan activities and the responsibilities of functionaries at different stages in the implementation process. Awareness of the progress of the implementation of district plan through the Finance and Administration Committee
Monitoring and evaluation of developmental schemes which are being imple-mented by the Intermediate Panchayats and Village Panchayats	***Essential*** Knowledge of the concept of monitoring. Review of on-going development programmes with reference to block wise performance and identify the problems of the blocks that have contributed to poor performance. Understanding and knowledge of the reports of the subject committees
Administrative control over the staff appointed by the District Panchayat and Intermediate Panchayat and Village Panchayat or transferred staff of the state government under the Panchayat sector	***Essential*** Knowledge of Panchayat Raj Act and various rules and bye-laws made therein. Awareness concerning delegation of powers and functions to PRIs with reference to transfer of development functions and staff and their control.
To take all necessary steps to generate financial resources within the framework of powers accorded by law	***Essential*** Knowledge of the sources of panchayati raj finance including sources of income from taxes, etc.

Category: Chairperson, Vice-Chairperson and Chairperson Subject Committees

Core Characteristics of Tasks	Training Objectives
Convene, preside and conduct meetings of the District Panchayat: The order of the business usually is (1) approval of the minutes of the last meeting, (2) questions, (3) review of progress, if any, matters pertaining to urgent official business, (4) resolutions, (5) government communica-tions, (6) reports of the Subject Committees, (7) other business	***Essential*** Knowledge regarding conduct of business, resolution, establish-ment, account, budget and audit, etc. Controlling and coordinating the execution of programmes; supervising and guiding the working of constituent organs, dealing with factions and professional groups. ***Desirable*** Encourages free discussion, ensure equitable participation of the members. Safeguarding the rights of the minorities, the protecting officials and articulating the feeling of non-officials; maintain law, order and decorum in the meetings and regulating discussions.
Exercise supervision and control over the chief executive officer and through him all officers and other employees of the District Panchayat	***Essential*** Knowledge of responsibilities of elected representatives at the district level, including role and responsi-bilities of officials at the district level. Proper appreciation of the respective roles, mutual adjustments and developing of proper attitudes in official and non-official relationship. Securing harmonious relationship with officials and non-officials.
Powers of Chairman Subject Committee (a) Preside over the meetings of the subject committee	***Essential*** Knowledge of powers and functions of Subject Committees Knowledge of the financial and

(b) Access to records of the committee (c) Power to call for information and return Power to sanction schemes or work allotted to the committees Exercise overall supervision over the financial and executive administration of the District Panchayat and place before the District Panchayat all questions connected therewith.	executive powers of the Chairman, District Panchayat as provided in the Panchayat State Act. This also requires objective outlook and considerable human relationship skills.
Political skills	***Essential*** Official/non-official relationships; intra-party conflict; new member/senior member relations; handling constituents problems; media relations; the central/local government interface; possession of intimate knowledge about popular reaction.

Intermediate Panchayat

Category: Members of Intermediate Panchayat

Core Characteristics of Tasks	Training Objectives
To prepare the developmental schemes of the Intermediate Panchayat consolidating the schemes of economic and social justice of Village Panchayat for onward transmission to the District Panchayat	***Essential*** Knowledge of district planning; knowledge regarding objectives, contents and methodologies of block plan; familiarity with the concept of spatial planning; awareness between the various levels of administrative hierarchy or vertical linkages. ***Desirable*** Familiarity with the process of planning at the national/state levels.

To ensure the implementation of schemes and programmes of central/state governments of schemes undertaken from own resources and overseeing the implementation on the basis of guidelines, principles, orders and other necessary requirements	***Essential*** Understanding of the various parameters regarding implementation of development activities and the responsibilities of official functionaries at different stages in the implementation process; awareness of the progress in the implementation of block plan through the finances and administration committee, public opinion, various reports of the subject committees and administrative reports.
To take all necessary steps to generate financial resources within the framework of powers accorded by the law of central/state governments Identifying schemes of development requiring institutional finance	***Essential*** A thorough understanding of the sources of generation of finances as prescribed in the Panchayat Raj Act of the state. A thorough understanding of the modalities of various development programmes, eligibility for assistance under these programmes, pattern of financial assistance, in respect of specific schemes, administration of subsidy, requirements of institutional credit, knowledge of lending rates for long-term loans terms finances available for various schemes. ***Desirable*** Role of commercial banks and other financial institutions in the implementation of developmental schemes through an instrument of credit. Role of National Bank for Agriculture and Rural Development (NABARD) and its potential linked credit plan, integration of credit plans with district plans.

Preparation of annual budget	***Essential*** Knowledge of pattern of budgeting, budget procedures, norms for budgeting, allocation of budget, accounting procedure and audit.
To coordinate and guide Village Panchayat	***Essential*** Knowledge of the concept of coordination in the perspective of village plans and various coordination instrumentalities

Intermediate Panchayat

Category: Chairperson, Vice-Chairperson and Chairperson, Subject Committees

Core Characteristics of Tasks	Training Objectives
Convene and preside over and conduct meetings of the Intermediate Panchayat	***Essential*** Knowledge regarding conduct of business, resolution and procedural aspects of establishment, account, audit, budget, etc.
Exercise supervision and control over the chief executive officer and through him all officers and other employees of the Intermediate Panchayat	Knowledge of responsibilities of elected representatives, including role and responsibilities of officials. Proper appreciation of the respective roles, mutual adjustments and developing proper convention and attitudes in official and non-official relationship
Exercise overall supervision over the financial and executive administration of the Intermediate Panchayat and place before it all questions connected therewith.	Knowledge of officials and executives powers of the Chairman, Intermediate panchayats as provided in the state of Panchayati Raj Act. This also requires objective outlook and considerable human relationship skills.

Village Panchayat

Category: Members of Village Panchayat

Core Characteristics of Tasks	Training Objectives
Coordinate and consolidate plans for economic development and social justice and for its onwards trans-mission to Intermediate Panchayat	***Essential*** Knowledge of block planning; familiarity with objectives, contents and methodology of village plan. ***Desirable*** Familiarity with the process of planning at district and block levels
To identify the priorities of developmental schemes within its jurisdiction	***Essential*** Awareness of the developmental problems with respect to poverty and area development programmes of the village
Selection of beneficiaries of the poverty alleviation programmes	***Essential*** Knowledge of objectives, strategy, targets and beneficiaries of developmental programmes with reference to poverty alleviation
To take all necessary steps to generate financial resources within the framework of powers accorded by the law of the state government	***Essential*** Knowledge of sources of Panchayati Raj finance including sources of income from taxes and other revenues
Preparation of annual budget	***Essential*** Knowledge of pattern of budgeting, budget procedure, norms for budgeting, allocation of budget, accounting procedure and audit.
Monitoring and evaluation of poverty alleviation programmes	***Essential*** Knowledge of management information system for planning and implementation; review of poverty alleviation programmes on the basis of subject committee reports and public opinion

Village Panchayat

Category: Chairperson, Vice-Chairperson and Chairperson, Subject Committees

Core Characteristics of Tasks	Training Objectives
Be responsible for convening the meeting of Gram Sabha and Village Panchayat and preside over its meetings Be responsible for the maintenance of the records of the Village Panchayat	*Essential* Knowledge regarding conduct of business, resolution, establishment, accounting, audit and budget, etc.
Have the general responsibility for the financial and executive administration of the Village Panchayat	Knowledge and responsibilities of elected representatives at village level, including roles and responsi-bilities of village level officials. Proper appreciation of the respective roles, mutual adjustments and developing proper conventions and attitude in the official and non-official relationship
Exercise administrative supervision and control over the work of the staff of the Village Panchayat	Knowledge of the financial and executive powers of the chairperson, Village panchayat, as provided in the state Panchayati Raj Act. This also requires objective outlook and considerable human relationship skills.

District Planning Committee

Category: Non-official Members of the District Planning Committee

Core Characteristics of Tasks	Training Objectives
Consolidation of plans prepared by Panchayati Raj Institutions and municipalities. To discuss and approve the Draft District Plan and	*Essential* Knowledge of multi-level planning; knowledge of decentralised planning: preparation of plans, identification of resources and data base; familiarity with objectives, contents and

submit it to the state government.	methodology; familiarity with the concept of spatial planning, understanding of the issues of rural urban interface and understanding of developing linkages to integrate the plans of the rural and urban area ***Desirable*** Familiarity with the process of planning at the national and state levels
Estimation of financial resources for financing the district plan	***Essential*** Familiarity with the development programmes; knowledge of resource allocation of various programmes: infrastructure, services oriented sector, poverty alleviation; familiarity with financial flow from state sources, central sources, inter-national agencies, local bodies, etc. in development schemes.
Allocation of sectoral and sub-sectoral outlays within the overall framework of the district development plan	***Essential*** Knowledge of broad objectives, strategy, targets, etc., of sectoral programmes, criteria for allocation to the blocks.
Identifying schemes of development requiring institutional finance	***Essential*** A thorough understanding of the modalities of various developmental programmes, eligibility for assistance under these programmes, pattern of financial assistance in respect of specific schemes, administration of subsidy, requirements of institutional credit, knowledge of the lending rates for long term loans-terms finances available for various schemes

	Desirable Role of commercial banks and other financial institutions in the implementation of developmental schemes through an instrument of credit. Role of NABARD and its potential linked credit plan, integration of credit plans with district plans.
To prepare the district budget	***Essential*** Knowledge of pattern of budgeting, budgetary procedure, norms for budgeting, allocation of budget, accounting procedure and audit. ***Desirable*** Familiarity with the rules governing formulation of the budget
Monitoring, Evaluation and Review of progress	***Essential*** Knowledge of basic concepts of monitoring and evaluation; knowledge of management information system for planning and implementation; application of computers for data management; review of development programmes on the basis of subject committee reports, instructions, expenditure, physical targets and study of public opinion.
Making suggestions to the state government with regard to the state sector schemes having significant bearing on the process of development of the district	***Essential*** Review of on-going development programmes with reference to block wise performance and identify the problems of the blocks that have contributed to poor performance.

Training Programmes Proposed

After having identified the training objectives on the basis of core characteristics of tasks relating to District Panchayat, Intermediate Panchayat, Village Panchayat and District Planning Committee, it is proposed to provide the outline of the training programmes for the above mentioned categories. Besides, an effort has also been made to understand the training needs of the members of the Gram Sabha and a course curriculum outline has also been prepared for them. It is important to underline that the design of training programmes should be treated as suggestive and may change with experience.

In deciding upon the formal programmes of training, it is imperative to keep in mind the fact that the panchayati raj representatives at all levels are not engaged in the operational sense of the term in planning, implementation, supervision and monitoring of the programmes. However, they keep a watch and participate along with the officials who really perform all these activities. As such, it is necessary, for these representative to have a broad orientation and understanding of the various tasks which they have to oversee, so that they contribute in a meaningful manner (through debate and discussion) in these activities. As such, it is necessary that the representatives are all well-versed, both in terms of conceptual understanding as well as its practical implications.

It is also important to mention that only four broad categories of programmes are being designed for this purpose. No attempt has been made to segregate the office bearers of these institutions from the elected members at various levels. It is a well known fact that, by and large, each members is in one way or the other connected with the subject committees. Hence, the whole thrust is to treat each panchayati raj body in totality and no bifurcation has been made in terms of training programmes for members and office bearers at the same institutional level.

In designing these programmes, the whole thrust of the argument underscore the importance that the effectiveness of these institutions will depend on the understanding of the tasks and responsibilities in terms of knowledge, skills and attitudes. It is a formidable task because the magnitude is very large. A distinction has also to be made relating to the fact that at the district level and intermediate level, by and large, the elected panchayati raj representatives are literate, but the situation at the village panchayat level is totally different, where a major segment of representatives are either illiterate or semi-literate. This question involves pedagogical and methodological innovations in the training of representatives. It is also important to point out that the programmes which are being designed below flowing from training objectives does show that both conceptually and practically subjects which are to be taught are complex and require certain degree of experience and maturity in the trainers. Objectives of training programmes for district panchayat, intermediate panchayat, and village panchayat are common. Besides, the duration of the training programmes for the above categories also by and large of the same duration i.e. (3-5 days). The following are the objectives:

Objectives

- Develop understanding about the provision of the Constitution regarding panchayati raj as well as State Government Act, rules and executive orders regarding panchayati raj
- Develop capabilities in planning and implementation of development programmes

Proposed Training Programme

District Panchayat Members

Level of Participants: Chairperson, Vice-Chairperson and Members

Course Contents

Panchayati Raj

- Concept of self-government
- Characteristics of panchayati raj with reference to inter-panchayat relations

- Panchayat's funds and raising internal resources
- Account and audit: social audit
- Panchayat's relationship with the government: inspection and control
- Functions of standing committee
- Supervision and control over intermediate panchayats and village panchayats

Planning Process

- Planning at national and state levels
- Multi-level planning and decentralised planning
- District Planning and familiarity with spatial planning
- Understanding of the issues of rural-urban interface
- District Planning: objectives, content and methodology

Development Programmes and Coordination

- Familiarity with development programmes: infrastructure, service oriented and poverty alleviation, both in rural and urban areas
- Criteria for allocation of funds to intermediate panchayats
- Financial Institutions in development schemes and requirements of institutional credit
- Familiarity and knowledge of rules governing the formulation of the district budget
- Panchayati raj system and inter-tier relationship
- Administrative structure for district planning
- Understanding of development linkages to integrate the plans of rural and urban areas

Monitoring, Evaluation and Review of Progress

- Knowledge of the concept of monitoring and evaluation
- Knowledge of management information system for planning and implementation
- Application of computers for data management

Procedural Aspects

- Holding of meetings

- Recording and dispatch of procedures
- No confidence motion
- Appointments, transfers, disciplinary act
- Purchases

Intermediate Panchayat Members

Level of Participants: Chairperson, Vice-Chairperson and Members

Course Contents

Panchayati Raj

- Concept of self-government
- Characteristics of panchayati raj with reference to inter-panchayat relations
- Panchayat's fund and raising internal resources
- Account and audit: social audit
- Panchayats relationship with the government: inspection and control
- Functions of standing committee
- Supervision and control over Village panchayats

Planning Process

- District Planning: Objectives, content and methodology

Development Programmes and Coordination

- Familiarity with development programmes: infrastructure, service oriented and poverty alleviation
- Criteria for allocation of funds to Village Panchayats
- Financial Institutions in development schemes and requirements of institutional credit
- Familiarity and knowledge of rules governing the formulation of the budget
- Panchayati raj system and inter-tier relationship
- Administrative structure for block planning
- Understanding of development linkages to integrate the plans of rural and urban areas

Monitoring and Evaluation and Review of Progress

- Knowledge of the concept of monitoring and evaluation
- Knowledge of management information system for planning and implementation
- Application of computers for data management

Procedural Aspects

- Holding of meetings
- Recording and dispatch of procedures
- No confidence motion
- Appointments, transfers, disciplinary act
- Purchases

Village Panchayat Members

Level of Participants: Sarpanch and Panch

Course Contents

Panchayati Raj

- Concept of self-government
- Characteristics of panchayati raj with reference to inter-panchayat relations
- The Panchayats relationship with the government: inspection and control
- Functions of subject committees
- Functions of Intermediate Panchayati with reference to planning and implementation
- Role and Responsibilities of officials at the village level
- Relationship between officials and elected representatives
- Collective leadership and people's participation

Procedural Aspects

- Holding of meetings
- Recording and dispatch of procedures
- No confidence motion
- Appointments, transfers, disciplinary action
- Purchases

Development Programmes

- Familiarity with the development programmes
- Role of financial banks and other financial institutions in the implementation of the development schemes
- Understanding of the budget
- Panchayat's fund and raising internal resources
- Account and Audit: social audit

Planning

- Knowledge and understanding with reference to objectives, contents and methodologies of the village plan
- Poverty alleviation programmes and area development programmes – procedures, beneficiaries and allocation of funds
- Sources of panchayati raj finance
- Monitoring, review and evaluation of programmes
- Developing common understanding with officials about the planning, approaches, and objectives

District Planning Committee Members

Objectives

- To gain an understanding about the district planning, policies, approaches, objectives, etc.
- To develop familiarity with the development programmes their monitoring and evaluation
- Understanding of preparation of budget and role of financial institutions in the implementation of the development schemes.

Course Contents

Planning Process

- Planning at national and state levels
- Multi-level planning and decentralised planning
- District planning and familiarity with spatial planning
- Issues of rural-urban interface
- District Planning: objectives, content and methodology

Development Programmes and Coordination

- Familiarity with development programmes: infrastructure, service oriented and poverty alleviation, both in rural and urban areas.
- Criteria for allocation of funds to blocks and municipal wards
- Financial institutions in development schemes and requirements of institutional credit
- Familiarity and knowledge of rules governing the formulation of the district budget
- Panchayati Raj system and inter-tier relationship
- Administrative structure for district planning
- Understanding of developing linkages to integrate the plans to rural and urban areas

Monitoring and Evaluation

- Knowledge of concept of monitoring and evaluation
- Knowledge of management information system for planning and implementation
- Application of computers for data management

Gram Sabha

The institution of Gram Sabha has been in existence in many states since 1947. However, it did not function well. "Our experience is that even in those States where the institution of the Gram Sabha has been introduced by Statutes as early as 1947, it cannot be said that the institution has been functioning there in any real sense of the term. Generally, these Gram Sabha meetings are thinly attended, and quorum is seldom achieved."[13] The Constitution (Seventy-third) Amendment Act, has recognised the Gram Sabha as a statutory unit under Article 243(G). It is defined as a body consisting of persons registered in the electoral rolls relating to a village comprised within the area of Panchayats at the village level. In most states, the functions of Gram Sabha are limited to discussion of annual statement of accounts, administrative reports and selection of beneficiaries of the anti poverty programmes. Some state like Haryana, Punjab and Tamil Nadu provide power of approval of budget to Gram Sabhas also. By and large, in states like Bihar, Karnataka, Kerala, Rajasthan, Punjab, Sikkim and Uttar Pradesh the Gram Sabha also undertakes programme for adult education and family welfare within the village. Similarly, in Bihar, Karnataka, Kerala, Rajasthan, Punjab, Sikkim, West Bengal and Tamil Nadu, Gram Sabhas also promote unity and harmony among all sections of society. In Haryana and Kerala, Gram Sabhas also consider and scrutinise existing schemes and all kinds of activities of panchayats; maintain a complete register of all developmental works undertaken by Gram Panchayat or by any other government department and scrutinise the completed works and all kinds of activities of the Gram Panchayat. It has been made incumbent on the Gram Sabha to hold at least two meetings in the financial year. The institution of Gram Sabha and its two minimum number of meetings are considered basic to the functioning of the panchayats. The first meeting of the Gram Sabha has to consider some important documents or matters such as the annual statement of accounts, the administrative report for the preceding year, development and other programmes proposed for the current financial year, the last audit note and the replies made thereto, etc. It is also to be recognised that the institution of Gram Sabha is commendable from the point of view of the democratic process. However, it has developed a number of weaknesses. Firstly, the Gram Sabhas are not meeting as often as they ought to according to the provisions of the law. Secondly, whenever meetings are held, the attendance is poor and, in some cases, the meetings are stage-managed and exist on paper only as there is no actual assemblage of the villagers at such meetings. Thirdly, even when meetings are actually convened, the transactions are conducted in a casual and half-hearted manner. The level of awareness and exposure among Gram Sabha members are very low. It has been pointed out that "There is an urgent need to break the culture of silence, as well as involve the Gram Sabhas in capacity building, sensitization and orientation to improve the grassroots scenario."[14] The most critical aspect of the Gram Sabha and its working in the true spirit as envisaged in the Constitution has far reaching implications. Some of the important implications are "The political education of the masses, larger participation in development programmes, better control over Panchayat leadership, better responsiveness of the administration, better mobilisation of resources and better care of public property..."[15]

Gram Sabha

Category: Members of Gram Sabha

Characteristics of Tasks	Training Objectives
Discuss report on the administration of the preceding year	Knowledge of basic principles of the PRIs. Awareness of the developmental programmes with reference to poverty alleviation
Examine annual statement of accounts and audit report	Knowledge of pattern of budgeting, allocation of budget, account procedure and audit.
Review programme of work for the year or any new programme	Knowledge of source of panchayati raj finance including sources of income
Select schemes, beneficiaries and locations	Knowledge of objectives, strategy, targets and beneficiaries of developmental programmes with reference to poverty alleviation and area development.

Awareness Camps

Level of Participants: Members of the Gram Sabha

Objectives

- Develop understanding about the State Panchayati Raj Act
- Develop capabilities regarding rights and duties of the Gram Sabha

Course Contents

- Concept of self-government
- Role and responsibilities of officials at the village level
- Collective leadership and people's participation
- Familiarity with the development programmes

- Poverty alleviation programmes and area development programmes – procedures, beneficiaries and allocation of funds

REFERENCES

1. India. Ministry of Rural Development. Department of Rural Development. (Panchayati Raj Division), 2001. *Report of The Task Force on Devolution of Powers and Functions Upon Panchayati Raj Institutions*. New Delhi. p. 5.
2. India. *Report of The Eleventh Finance Commission (For 2000-2005)*. June 2000. p. 83.
3. Ibid. p. 83.
4. Ibid. p. 83.
5. India. 2001. Report of The Task Force on Devolution of Powers and Functions Upon Panchayati Raj Institutions. *op. cit*.
6. Ibid. Annexure-V. pp. 55-82.
7. Ibid. Annexure-VI. pp. 83-127.
8. India. Lok Sabha. Thirty-Seventh Report, Standing Committee on Urban and Rural Development, 2002. Ministry of Rural Development, (Department of Rural Development). Implementation of Part IX of the Constitution. New Delhi: Lok Sabha Secretariat, p. 19.
9. India. Lok Sabha. Thirty Seventh Report. Standing Committee on Urban and Rural Development. 2002. op.cit. p. 18.
10. India. 2001. Report of The Task Force on Devolution of Powers and Functions Upon Panchayati Raj Institutions. op.cit. p. 21.
11. India. 2001. Report of The Task Force on Devolution of Powers and Functions Upon Panchayati Raj Institutions. *op. cit*. pp. 21-23 and 32-33.
12. India. 2001. Report of The Task Force on Devolution of Powers and Functions Upon Panchayati Raj Institutions. *op. cit*. p. 10. See also India. Planning Commission. 2000. Mid Term Appraisal of Ninth Five Year Plan (1997-2002). New Delhi. pp. 176-177 and The State of the Panchayats: A Mid Term Review and Appraisal, 22 November 2006, Vol. III, Ministry of Panchayati Raj, Government of India, p. 452.
13. Joshi, G.V. 1995. Gram Sabha in Karnataka: A Non-Starter?. Kurukshetra, 43(7), April, p. 113.
14. Yatindra Singh. 2002. Decentralized Governance in Madhya Pradesh: Experiences of the Gram Sabha in Scheduled Areas. Economic and Political Weekly, 37(40), 5 October, p. 4103.
15. Jain, S.C. 1967. Community Development and Panchayati Raj in India, Bombay: Allied Publishers. p. 168.

5

Training of Panchayati Raj Elected Representatives

Organisation and Management Perspective

It is a fact that mere institution of people's representatives can be no asset. A programme of training has, therefore, to be organised, all along the line. There is an imperative need of making the elected representatives in these democratic and popular institutions conscious of their basic rights and responsibilities. The PRIs need to develop close relationships with the administration on the one hand and the people on the other, thereby making the administration, development oriented and people oriented.

The primary concern in the training of elected representatives is to enhance the effectiveness of rural leadership through an organised process of learning. Training has to be used systematically to develop the capabilities of the elected representatives at the village, block and district levels. However, it is necessary to analyse some basic conditions on which an all-India wide programme of training of elected representatives should be based:

- Firstly, programme of training of elected representatives should be planned and implemented with a full awareness and understanding that it is an important condition for the success of PRIs.
- Secondly, the magnitude of training requirements for elected representatives is very sizeable. There are at

present, 537 district panchayats, 6097 intermediate panchayats and 234676 village panchayats in the country. As such, it has to be conducted in a decentralised manner. It must also be flexible, so as to adapt to the local and regional context. This effort also requires constant attention and follow-up at the higher level.

- Thirdly, such a programme must be a collaborative venture among the union/state governments, universities/colleges, and professional training institutions, and voluntary organisations. Each of these have a special background and facilities which make them best equipped to conduct particular phases of professionally oriented programme.
- Fourthly, the success of Constitution (Seventy-third) Amendment in both letter and spirit, depends to a large extent, on designing and successfully conducting such training programmes.
- Fifthly, the training programmes should seek to improve rural leadership in knowledge and awareness, skills and sensitivity to the values and interests of the society. These programmes should also develop in the elected representatives a proper understanding to achieve cooperation with the officials on the one side and the public on the other.
- Sixthly, such programmes should widen the horizon of the rural leadership to make them aware of the social and economic problems, problems of inequality, problems relating to social justice, etc.

These are some of the challenges which will have to be kept in mind while organising the training programmes for elected representatives of the PRIs.

The analysis of the panchayati raj training in the during 1959-69 and 1970-2006 has shown a large number of infirmities and weaknesses in terms of: institutional structure, syllabi, training of trainers, methodology of training, absenteeism of the participants, deficient training material, etc. Since 1993, the task has become more daunting and formidable not only because of the magnitude of the problem, but also due to the fact that around 60 per cent of the representatives at each level are from the weaker sections of society. Although no all-India picture is available regarding the training imparted in different states to these representatives, however, the case study conducted in Madhya Pradesh, had amply shown that the training is deficient in a number of ways. As a matter of fact, we are repeating the same mistakes again and again. By and large, except the training of district panchayat members and some training at the intermediate panchayat level, not much effort has gone into the training of village panchayat representatives.

The Ministry of Rural Development, Government of India, by and large, concentrated in the beginning i.e. during 1993 to 1994 on the training of trainers at the national level institutions like National Institute of Rural Development, Indian Institute of Public Administration, National Academy of Administration and building of panchayati raj training material. Besides, providing a meagre allocation to different states for strengthening existing training infrastructure. The Government of India has also not evolved any training policy for the panchayati raj. There has been ad-hocism in its approach towards the training of panchayati raj representatives. At the state level, except in West Bengal there has been no clarity regarding the training.

This analysis clearly underscores the need for looking into the problem of training from a different perspective. The conventional framework of providing panchayat raj training through state training institutions like ATI, SIRD and ETC has serious limitations as their capacity to fulfil this task is very limited. Besides, the backlog of training of development functionaries is so much that these institutions are not even in a position in the context of panchayati raj to train the elected representatives. The SIRDs and ETCs are also deficient in terms of limited academic support and training infrastructure, etc. Most of the faculty positions in ETCs remain vacant in most of the states. It has to be made clear that, out of nearly 3 million panchayati raj representatives to be trained, hardly five per cent have to be trained at the district panchayat and intermediate panchayat levels and the rest 95 per cent to be trained in around (2.50 lakh) village panchayats. This calls for a new strategy. There is a need that some kind of legal provision be made for this purpose. All state government panchayati raj statutes should make provision for training. In the absence of this, the training will remain an ad-hoc and cosmetic exercise, which it has been since the last 40 years.

After having analysed the training of elected panchayati raj representatives, since 1959 to 2006 as well as the training programmes at all the levels (outlining the course design), it is necessary to estimate the magnitude of the training requirements involved in this task. This will help us to decide: the role of the Union and State Governments, planning and organisational requirements of training at the district level and below, the training organisations, the trainers, the format and content of training programmes, the question of pedagogy, training techniques, duration, location and frequency of training programmes at various levels and finance, etc. This chapter will look into all these aspects systematically so as to provide a framework of the training elected panchayati raj representatives. It is necessary for this purpose, first to appreciate the magnitude of the task of training requirements. If we look at Table-7, which gives a state-wise list of figures available at all the levels, we will find that it is a very formidable task. The table below gives a picture of the number of elected representatives at village panchayat, intermediate panchayat and district panchayat levels:

Magnitude of Training

Out of approximately 30 lakh (see Table-7 for state-wise profile) total number of elected representatives as on April, 2004, approximately 28,97,363 are at the village panchayat level. Approximately 50 per cent representatives at the village panchayat level are from SCs, STs and women. This is the most critical component in the training of elected representatives. Similarly, at the intermediate panchayat level, the total number is 1,55,164. Out of this, approximately 50 per cent are from the

Number of Panchayati Raj Institutions and their Elected Representatives as on April, 2004

Panchayats	*Nos*	*Total No. of elected representatives (%age)*				
		Gen.	*SC*	*ST*	*Women*	*Total*
Village Panchayat	234676	1479369 (51.05)	346002 (11.95)	233765 (8.06)	838227 (28.94)	2897363 (100.00)
Intermediate Panchayat	6097	77166 (49.73)	22333 (14.39)	8210 (5.29)	47455 (30.59)	155164 (100.00)
District Panchayat	537	8067 (48.86)	2201 (13.32)	1322 (8.00)	4923 (29.82)	16513 (100.00)
Total:		1564602 (50.99)	370536 (12.07)	243297 (7.93)	890605 (29.01)	3069040 (100.00)

Source: Ministry of Rural Development, Government of India, New Delhi, April, 2004

weaker sections. At the village panchayat level, these representatives are spread over in 2,34,676 village panchayats and at the intermediate panchayat level, their spread is in 6,097 such bodies. On the whole, it is a huge task both in terms of locations to be served and the numbers to be trained.

It is evident from these tables that the training of elected representatives at different levels is of considerable magnitude. These estimates indicate that, in view of the limited skills and training facilities available, it will be difficult even to meet a small portion of the training requirements at all the levels. It is important to emphasise that most of the training programmes at the village panchayat level and even at the intermediate panchayat level, are being run in collaboration with the Non Governmental Organisations (NGOs). However, all-India wise picture regarding the panchayati raj training programmes and their achievements in different states at present is not available. The analysis made in the previous chapter about the training institutions, brought out that they are totally inadequate to meet these requirements. This, inturn, requires a new strategy for providing training facilities to the panchayati raj representatives.

The sheer magnitude of the training requirements also involves the question of training of trainers as well as the organisation of decentralised training programmes at the district and sub-district levels. As far as the question of training of trainers is concerned, it is important to note that there is a need for training the trainers in a number of areas like new panchayati raj set-up, decentralised planning, technical awareness about the functions assigned, problems of implementation and monitoring of development programmes, etc. There is also a need to identify the institutions which will provide conceptual and technical know-how to these trainers.

Institutional Arrangements

We have already seen that the existing government state training institutions engaged in rural development training are totally inadequate to provide training to the elected panchayat raj representatives as the magnitude of the task on the one hand and, on the other, the spread over of the panchayat institutions. It is necessary to look into the institutional arrangements, which need to be made to provide training to these representatives in an effective manner. Besides, the existing government state training institutions are occupied in the training of the state and district level officials. They do not possess the necessary infrastructure to impart this type of training. As such, there is a need to look into a different institutional arrangements. For this purpose, it is necessary to emphasise that since the last fifty years, there has been phenomenal development of education in India.

It is relevant to point out that as far as back in 1919, the Hartog Committee recommended "The universities have responsibilities not only to their students but also to the country at large"[1] and pleaded that extension work should be an integral part of the university system. Similarly, the University Education Commission, chaired by Dr. S. Radhakrishnan, recommended the integration of the educational system with the problems of rural life and facilitating and contributing to improving rural conditions. The University Education Commission also emphasised the need of education for social emancipation. For this purpose, it recommended the basic education programme, the people's college and setting up of rural universities. The idea of people's college was taken from Denmark. It was pointed out in the report that the people's colleges have played a significant role in their development "from ignorance and poverty to about the highest general level of education and well-being of all the peoples of the earth"[2]. Besides, the report of the Secondary Education Commission, chaired by Dr. A. Lakshmanaswami Mudaliar, emphasised the need for re-orienting the educational system in such a way "that it will stimulate a cultural renaissance"[3]. This committee also emphasised the need for developing democratic citizenship and pleaded for the training of the citizen. To this end, the committee stressed the need to develop the "capacity for clear thinking and a receptivity to new ideas"[4] and development of the scientific attitude of mind. Similarly, the Kothari Commission, in 1964-66, also advocated the need for the universities to help in the social economic and cultural growth of the community which they serve and the existing educational system particularly the universities can provide effective leadership in this task.[5] Likewise ignorance can be eliminated by the pooling of our educational resources, "The system of education must provide for the interplay of forces from the village school to the university"[6].

Resource Persons

As in 1994-95, there were approximately 2 lakh teachers in the colleges and universities in India dealing with general education. There are 7,55,798 teachers in India at the level of higher secondary school/colleges and out of this, 2,25,120 are women (Table 9). At the high/post basic school, the number of teachers is around 10 lakh, out of which more than 1/3rd are women and 90 per cent of the teachers are trained (Table 10).

It is significant to point out that all over the country there is a large segment of retired persons spread all over the country who could play a significant role in the training of panchayati raj representatives. These persons are from technical, non-technical, developmental, and from banks, accounts departments, etc. With some orientation all these superannuated persons could act as excellent trainers. There is a large banking system available in the country and the network has reached the villages and the staff of banking system could also be utilised for the purpose of training.

This calls for a new institutional set-up for the training of panchayati raj representatives. Before we elaborate on this point, it has to be recognised that the training modules formulated in the previous chapter clearly enunciate, a course curriculum at each level, which is formidable in terms of knowledge, skills, procedural and behavioural components. It is suggested that the existing educational system should be drawn in the mainstream of the training of panchayati raj representatives. It is important to mention that during the early sixties, the training structure was created for panchayati raj representatives, the general educational support system in the country was not of the order to cater for this type of requirement. However, over the last more than 50 years, a huge educational infrastructure is available in the country to support training of panchayati raj representatives in a decentralised manner. For example, there are 198 universities for general education in the country. There are approximately 8,000 colleges for general education and approximately 1,26,000 high school/ higher secondary/intermediate/pre-degree junior colleges in the country and about 800 teachers training colleges (Table-8). In fact, most of the divisional and regional set-up at the state level, by and large, are having a university. Almost all the districts and blocks in the country have colleges for general education. Similarly, as mentioned earlier, 1,60,000 high school or junior colleges are available at district, block and sub-block levels. All these institutions are involved in general education. It is suggested that the universities, located at the divisional/ regional headquarters, should be drawn in the mainstream of panchayati raj training by providing training to master trainers. Almost all the topics mentioned in the previous training curriculum are covered by and large in an university syllabi at the graduate and post-graduate levels. The teachers are fully conversant with the technical details as well as conceptual and practical aspects of these problems. They are also conversant, being at the divisional/regional headquarters, about the problems and the issues in terms of socio, political and economic aspects. The medium of instruction in most of the universities is the regional language which will be of great value.

The university system has close links with the constituent colleges and teachers and is in complete knowhow of the discipline-wise availability of teachers and also has the competence to identify teachers who can act resource persons in the training of panchayati raj functionaries. The structure of the divisional/regional set-up is available at least all over the country. This structure of divisional/regional set-up will not only provide the university system, which will function, as mentioned earlier, as a nodal agency, for providing academic inputs but also a place where there is availability of senior officials of almost all the departments of the state. As such, the divisional/regional headquarters will provide a pool of resource persons drawn from academic community on the one side and senior officials on the other, who can act as faculty, for the training of master trainers as well as training of elected panchayati raj representatives.

Coordination Committee

It is necessary for this purpose to set up at the divisional/regional level a Coordination Committee consisting of the following:

Chairman, District Planning Committee	Chairman
Divisional Commissioner or Equivalent Authority	Member
University Dean Social Sciences	Member
Additional Director/Joint Director (Higher Education)	Member
Joint Director, Panchayat	Member-Secretary

The purpose of this committee will be to:

- Identify master trainers from the relevant disciplines, (political sciences, public administration, economics, sociology and geography) from the university or colleges.

- Identify relevant senior or retired officials who will act as master trainers for training relating to matters of technical details (development programmes, planning, audit and accounts, procedures), etc.
- Identify from the constituent colleges trainers/resource persons.
- Provide training to non-official members of District Planning Committee (to cater the needs of the constituent districts).
- Provide training to master trainers and district level trainers.

The administrative aspects in terms of venue of the training, administrative support in terms of infrastructure, date and duration, financial aspect will be looked by the Joint Director Panchayat.

- The training programme should be organised during the lean period.
- A suitable honorarium should be given to resource persons. The committee will also be free to utilise the services of retired officials or social workers.
- It will be the duty of the Joint Director Panchayat (as member-secretary) to prepare a training calender in advance before the commencement of the financial year for all the levels.
- All outstation participants should be provided boarding and lodging facilities including conveyance to and fro for the duration of the programme. (At the divisional/regional headquarters, there is no dearth of suitable venue for the programme).
- This committee will also look into the monitoring and evaluation of training programmes both in the area of training of district planning committee members and training of master trainers.

The training of resource persons (master trainers) will be conducted by the university. The purpose of short training programmes for the master trainers will be to provide them intensive training in the area of governance, Constitution (Seventy-third) Amendment Act, various developmental programmes, roles and responsibilities at different levels of panchayat system, the mandatory functions of the panchayats and inter-relationship with panchayats, district planning, spatial planning, the operational aspects of district plans, etc. The university system, which at present is insulated from the panchayat raj, will provide a certain kind of closeness which will help not only in the training of the panchayati raj representatives but also can be drawn in the process of district planning. It will also be the function of this committee to identify the refresher courses or workshops on different issues of panchayati raj.

District Level Coordination Committee

There is also a need to constitute a committee at the district level consisting of the following:

President, District Panchayat	Chairman
Chairman, Standing Committee (Administration and Finance)	Member
District Collector	Member
Chief Executive Officer (Panchayat)	Member
District Education Officer	Member
District Panchayat Officer	Member-Secretary

The role of the above committee will be to organise training programmes for the district panchayat members, the resource persons will be drawn from the academic side on the basis of the selection made by the divisional committee. A similar exercise will be undertaken for providing technical inputs in terms of development programmes procedures, accounts and audit. This committee will also identify resource persons, drawn from academic side (located in the district or in the blocks to act as resource persons for block level panchayati raj representatives). For each block, there should be one institution tied for this purpose. The role of the member-secretary will be to arrange for training: venue, duration, time schedule, course curriculum, etc. As mentioned earlier, there are nearly 7,800 colleges for general education in the country. It should not be difficult to identify such institutions which can serve the purpose of at least one block. It is necessary to emphasise that the committee should be free to invite resource persons even outside the administrative machinery i.e. retired persons and also from voluntary organisations, social workers, etc. The training of representatives of intermediate panchayat will be conducted at the block headquarters or nearby suitable place (looking into the location of the college or some central point which will be convenient from the point of view of providing training to panchayati raj representatives of more than one block). This training for panchayati raj representatives will be planned, coordinated and decided by the district coordinating committee.

Intermediate Level Coordination Committee

A similar committee will be constituted at the intermediate level consisting of the following:

President, Intermediate Panchayat	Chairman
Chairman, Standing Committee (Administration and Finance)	Member
Sub-Divisional Officer	Member
District Education Officer	Member
Block Development Officer	Member-Secretary

The purpose of he committees will be the following:

- To identify the educational institutions and the resource persons both from administrative and academic community, social workers, etc.
- To identify the location of the training programme and provide training infrastructure.
- The resource persons should be given honorarium plus conveyance to and fro, etc. which should be decided by the committee. Even the official members should get honorarium.
- The resource persons for the purpose of gram panchayat training should be trained by the resource persons at the district level.

- It will also monitor and evaluate and send reports about the training
- Most of the resource persons should be drawn from high school/intermediate/pre-degree junior colleges and there are around 1,26,000 such colleges all over the country.
- While organising these programmes, efforts should be made to see that their organised during lean seasons because most of the members from the weaker sections (Scheduled Castes/Scheduled Tribes/women) belong to socio-economic groups which are landless and daily wagers. At least the representative attending this training should be given not only boarding and lodging (if necessary), but also conveyance allowance. The duration of the course at all levels should not be more than 5 days.
- The training at all levels should be compulsory.
- On the basis of evaluation of the programme, periodic training should also be organizsd as refresher courses in the areas like planning, procedures, accounts etc.

Organisation and Administration

At the Government of India level, there is a need to constitute a committee consisting of representatives from Ministries of Panchayati Raj (PR), Human Resource Development (HRD), Rural Development (RD), Information and Broadcasting (IB) and the University Grants Commission (UGC). Its functions would be: (1) to advise government, at the centre and at the states, on all matters relating to training of elected panchayati raj representatives and drawing up suitable policies, plan and programmes for their consideration, (2) to ensure adequate coordination between officials and non-officials agencies, (3) to review from time to time the progress made and to formulate suggestions for changes and improvements, (4) to ensure necessary funding and finances for the programme of this magnitude, and (5) to promote research and evaluation of the training programmes.

Similar bodies should be setup at the state level and the

role of these bodies will be to provide overall policy, plans and necessary funds. However, both at the union and the state levels there is a need for a coordinating committees, consisting of departmental heads, concerned with various aspect of training programme. At the state level, the functions of the committee of the officials should be – (1) to frame qualifications of the teaching staff, (2) to look into the syllabus of different courses of training programmes, (3) to frame rules for incentives, duration, periodicity of training programmes, (4) to provide necessary funds for conducting these programmes, and (5) preparation of syllabus for training of trainers, etc.[8]

Finance

The finance for training of panchayati raj representatives will depend on the training objectives, periodicity of training, numbers to be trained each year, duration of training, the type of training, the methodology of training and the location aspects of training. To illustrate, during the year 1994, the Government of West Bengal pooled up the financial resources made available by the UNICEF, Government of India and the state government and allotted to all the districts for training purposes on a scale of Rs.6,900 for each training course of 18 hours for 40 participants on an average. The expenditure heads comprised: messing charges of participants and resources persons and supporting staff at the cost of Rs. 30 per day for 3 days, honorarium at the cost of Rs. 50/- per lecture hour for 18 such hours and the rest for contingency charges.[7] However, in the context of the village and intermediate panchayat and even district panchayat, it is necessary to see that the persons who are below the poverty line may also be given the minimum wages applicable in that area for attending the programme each day. This incentive is necessary for encouraging them to participate in the programme.

The Ministry of Rural Development, Government of India is spending a considerable amount of money in the poverty related programmes both (area- specific and for people below the poverty line) as well as providing financial assistance for infrastructure development, minimum needs, social assistance, etc. The Twelfth Finance Commission to augment the consolidated funds of the states recommended grants-in-aid of Rs. 20,000 crore to the panchayats for the period 2005-10 (Table 12). There are a number of developmental programmes of other departments both of the Union Government and State Governments in which during 2000-2001, approximately Rs. 72,000 crore were allocated (Tables 11 and 11A). In the light of the above, it is suggested that the Government of India consider prescribing a percentage of the budget of the allocations made in rural development and related areas (as mentioned in XIth Schedule) to be allocated to the training of elected representatives. Looking at the magnitude of the task of training at least one per cent of the total budget of the programmes for each year must be made available for the training purpose. A suitable mechanism must be evolved to ensure that these funds are actually made available and spent for training. It should also be ensured that no money is spent on the capital expenditure. The break-up of training should be on the following: boarding and lodging/TA/DA charges of the participants; cost of preparation of the background material; audio-visual aids, honorarium to guest faculty, and other office expenses.

Training of Trainers

The choice of resources persons is important. For this purpose, the system should be flexible enough to allow the cooperation of professionals from various fields. As pointed out earlier, there are a large number of areas from where trainers or resource persons can be drawn: teachers from the universities/colleges and higher secondary schools, serving or retired officials of various development departments, people from NGOs, banking staff and cooperative sector staff as well as leaders of political parties. There is a need to train them so as to make them suitable for the purpose of training. A substantial investment would have been to be made for preparing them as effective trainers.

Another aspect relates to the proper monetary incentive to the trainers. The remuneration to be paid to these persons should be made on some realistic basis which should not only provide them proper financial incentive but also a sense of pride.

The methodology adopted for training of trainers also needs to be looked into carefully. By and large, every programme of training of trainers should be in the nature of workshop. These workshops should not only inculcate in the trainers, the methods of training to be used but also the preparation of instructional and other materials. Attention should be given to solve the trainer's problems. The emphasis in the training of trainers programme should be to sustain their interest.

The training programmes should have two essential components ; (a) it must as far as possible, be based and aimed at developing right attitudes and imparting skills and information which will help the panchayati raj leaders to undertake their responsibilities in an effective manner, and (b) it must help the illiterate, the weaker sections, including women, to integrate themselves in the larger context of panchayat raj as well as to participate effectively in social and political life of the locality.

Training Methods

The training of panchayati raj leaders or representatives requires many enabling conditions for the effective organisation of these programmes. One important consideration relates to the fact that, at least at the village panchayat leve,l most of them are from weaker sections and besides the literacy level is poor, and in case of women in particular, they are custom and tradition bound, and have hardly any political experience. Besides, there is a mandatory provision for the representatives of these groups to hold chairperson's position by rotation. All this calls for right kind of methods of training. As a matter of fact, it is imperative for evolving training methods that are sensitive to the needs of an illiterate adult learner.

In building up methods of training, it is necessary to relate them with the objective of the training programes. In fact, not only right methods of training are required but also the right kind of trainers. The methods of training should not be regarded merely as a device adopted for communicating certain items of information to the panchayati raj leaders but is a complex task of creating awareness, knowledge, attitude, skills and values.

In training methods, by and large, there is over emphasis on lecture method alone. Mostly, at the village level and intermediate panchayat level and atleast for a large segment of the members who are drawn from vulnerable groups SC/ST and women, it must be kept in mind that this method alone will not be able to communicate the skills and knowledge needed for these persons. There is a need for specialised educational institutions like National Council of Educational Research and Training (NCERT) and National Institute of Educational Planning and Administration (NIEPA) or a department of education of a University to go into this problem of method of training in the context of rural India. These institutions, while developing the right kind of methods, should look into the reality of their background as well as suitably devise methods which could provide them the understanding of the procedures, the programmes, planning, inter-personal relationships, capacity for clear thinking, capacity to judge issues and problems, etc. In this connection, the widest use should be made of the mass media of communication for awakening, sustaining the interest of the trainees and also for giving them general support through-out the training programme. All forms of the electronic media should be utilised for creating and maintaining an atmosphere which will be conducive for the success of this programme. Such programmes should be carefully planned with due regard to local conditions and requirements. Besides, All India Radio and television should be used for awakening the trainees towards their responsibilities to civic life and to the national development programmes. The thrust should be to devise methods of training which will hold the interest of the elected representatives. The approach in a way should be in planning the methods of training not only to focus on knowledge to be imparted but also on the thoroughness with which it is acquired by the trainers.

The training programmes should be conducted in a methodical and scientific manner so as to provide a right orientation in the trainees. The emphasis should be to reduce the complexity of the lectures and the training programme should be scrutinised with the learner's receptivity, etc. While deciding on the syllabus, training methods and duration, etc., it is relevant to quote McLuhan who pointed out in the context of non-literate societies that we should not approach these societieis "with many of the expectations and patterns... acquired from... highly literate society."[8] This also holds true in the context of large percentage of illiterate representatives.

REFERENCES

1. Auxiliary Committee of the Indian Statutory Commission. (Chairman, Sir Philip Hartog) quoted in Syed Nurullah and J. P. Naik. 1951. *A History of Education In India.* (During the British Period), 2nd Edition. Bombay: Macmillan & Co. LTD. p. 645.
2. India. 1950. *The Report of The University Education Commission (December 1948-August 1949), Volume 1.* (Chairman: S. Radhakrishnan). p. 559.
3. India. Ministry of Education. 1953. *Report of The Secondary Education Commission (October 1952 – June 1953).* New Delhi. (Chairman: A. Lakshmanaswami Mudaliar). p. 23.
4. Ibid. p. 24.
5. India. Ministry of Education. 1967. *Report of The Education Commission, 1964-66 Education and National Development.* New Delhi. (Chairman: D. S. Kothari). p. 437.
6. Dey, S. K. 1961. *Panchayati Raj : A Synthesis.* New Delhi: Asia Publishing House. p. 106.
7. West Bengal. Directorate of Panchayats. 1994. Documenta-tion on West Bengal Panchayats. *Systematic Training of Elected Panchayat Members.* Calcutta. p. 7.
8. Stearn, Gerald Emanuel. 1967. Conversations with McLuhan. Encounter, 28(6). June. pp. 51-52. See also Mead Margaret. 1956. New Lives for Old-Cultural Transformation – Manus, 1928-1953. New York: William Morrow and Company. pp. 3-17.

6

A Policy Perspective

John Stuart Mill provided a framework for the role of local bodies in a democracy, the functions to be performed by these bodies, the relationship between officials and non-officials, etc. Mill is the only political thinker who gave a comprehensive conceptual framework of local bodies. His thinking is not confined alone to the role and responsibilities, but covers such important aspects as local bodies and the labouring classes, political education and training of the labouring classes, contents of the training programme, etc. Because of these aspects, Mill has still lot of relevance in the Indian context.

Political education of the elected members of local bodies has been one of the main objectives in the setting up of these institutions. It is with this high aim that these bodies were established by Lord Ripon in 1882. Participation in a modern democratic system at any level needs articulation, knowledge and understanding of the rules, regulations, laws and related aspects. In the absence of this knowledge and understanding, the participation of the illiterate member in the real sense is not possible. Only notionally the poor are members of the PRIs without fulfilling their role and responsibilities and obligations in a meaningful manner. Democracy entails making informed choices. It is not possible due to the illiteracy of a large number of elected representatives. This illiteracy is a product of elitist educational policy during the pre-independence period. However, this policy has remained with marginal changes in the post-Independence period also. The campaign of adult education, after independence did not make any dent in the situation. As a consequence, a large segment of the population mostly the marginalised section is illiterate. For democracy to be successful an enlightened citizenship is a must. However, this did not happen in India, as no effort was made to overcome this problem.

In the context of panchayati raj, a massive effort was made to train the emerging leadership in the rural India in the late 1950s. To fulfill this goal, a large number of institutions were hurriedly established. The objective was not confined to train elected panchayati raj representatives but also MPs and MLAs as well as adult citizens in the rural areas. As such, the magnitude of the task was very large as well as complex spread over in lakhs of villages and thousands of blocks and hundreds of districts of the country. This training programme was operated or about a decade i.e. from1959 to 1969. However, a number of problems were noticed: the institutions created for the training at the block and village levels were not effective; mostly the training was in urban areas devoid of rural surroundings, there was absenteeism, trainers were not upto the mark; there was no cognisance of the suitability of timing from the point of view of the participants; the course syllabus was not scientifically determined; the trainers lacked motivation as well as knowledge and deeper understanding of the panchayati raj, etc. The training methods were lecture-based and not also taking cognisance of the fact that a large chunk of the representatives were illiterate. To make them understand the nuances of governance, official and non-official relationship, budget, accounts, procedures, developmental programmes, requires a different kind of methodology. Besides, from 1970 to 1992, was a period of a comparative decline in the training of panchayati raj representatives. This fact was very prominently mentioned by Asoka Mehta Committee report as well as many other reports by the committees appointed in a large number of states. However, all these reports pointed out the need for the training of the elected representatives in a more scientific manner.

The analysis of the working of the local government has brought out again and again that development programmes have benefited the rich and the privileged. The weaker sections have not been able to gain in a significant manner partly because of the lack of their "linguistic capabilities". It has also to be seen from the perspective that since the Constitution (Seventy-third) Amendment the panchayati raj is intended to be seen more and more as a vehicle for the social and economic transformation. If the panchayati raj is being seen as a vehicle for social and economic transformation, then there is urgent need to 'break the culture' of silence. All the major reports dealing with the appraisal of the local self government bodies have unfailingly pointed out the lack of awareness and understanding, are the major factors in the decline of the panchayati raj as a vehicle for social and economic transformation. However, all these committees have pointed out the need for training of the elected representatives.

At present, the core training programmes at the state level, by and large, are handled by the Administrative Training Institutes and State Institute of Rural Development. However, the magnitude and spread over of the problem is so large that except in West Bengal, the emphasis has alone being on the training of district panchayat representatives. There is adhocism as for as the training of Intermediate Panchayat members and Village Panchayat members is concerned. The existing institutional arrangements are totally inadequate to provide training on a continuous basis to all the levels of panchayati raj. This inadequacy is reflected on the following factors:

- The existing training institutions do not have the capacity to arrange the training programmes on a continuous and regular basis.
- These institutions were basically set up to cater to the needs of training of governmental functionaries and the work load is so high that it is difficult for these institutions to cater to the needs of the elected panchayati raj representatives.
- There is a need also to give special attention for the training of the panchayat leaders particularly those belonging to weaker sections, women, Scheduled Castes, Scheduled Tribes and backward classes. This

section has not become assertive and they are not allowed to participate freely in the panchayat meetings. As such, in the training programmes, special attention has to be given to the training of the weaker sections. The existing institutional set-up is not attuned for this purpose.

- The sheer size of the task of the training of village panchayat level elected representatives is very large. The elected representatives at this level constitute around 95 per cent of the elected representatives in the entire panchayati raj system. In many of the states, they do not receive any training, however their role is of great significance. As a matter of fact, this tier of panchayat raj provide an interface with the citizens on the one hand and bring the problems of implementation of developmental programmes in a more intense manner.

All this calls for thinking on the subject and preparing a very comprehensive framework in all details i.e. course curricula at different levels, institutional arrangements for training, method of training, duration, periodicity incentives to the trainers and trainees, training of trainers, location of training, etc. In our context, there is a need for education for democracy which should form an important part right from the school education.

This study analyses in a scientific manner, on the basis of the responsibilities and the tasks of the elected representatives at different levels, the training needs at each level. On the basis of the analysis, an attempt has been made to prepare the syllabus for different levels of panchayati raj. It also include syllabus for the district planning committee and the Gram Sabha. Since 1993, almost more than 14 years have passed and two elections have already taken place of PRIs in most parts of the country. However, the training of panchayati raj representatives is still deficient in many ways. By and large, almost in all the states there has been training at least of district panchayat members, but except West Bengal probably no attempt has been made in a systematic manner to train the representatives at the village and at the intermediate level also.

The task of training is very complex because the numbers to be trained is very large, around three million. Out of this, about 95 per cent are the village panchayat level representatives. The existing institutions of training in terms of ATIs, SIRD and ETCs are totally inadequate to shoulder this responsibility. Partly because of these institutions are engaged in the training of officials, staff is not position at the ETC level, the infrastructure will not be able to take up such a load, etc. This requires a different type of institution arrangement to be successful. It is high time to bring the existing educational system in the country in the mainstream of the training of elected representatives. The higher secondary schools and the colleges in the country provide an excellent infrastructure in terms of teachers buildings, and other support system. There are around 10 lakh teachers at the higher secondary level with a large percentage of female teachers who are well qualified to undertake this task, at least for the village and at the intermediate level. What is needed is training of trainers by the universities and other institutions dealing in social sciences and public administration. This system has to be totally decentralised and the work of training should be undertaken by a committee at the district level comprising of people drawn from panchayat raj and university, district officials, etc. The committee should be in position at the intermediate level with very well defined functions and responsibilities. This system will provide flexibility in the syllabi. For this purpose, there is a need for the training of trainers, funding should be from the resources made available every year to the 29 subjects of XIth Schedule of the Constitution which are funded both by the central and various state governments. It is possible to reach and conduct the training of elected representatives in a meaningful manner by drawing the existing educational system in the mainstream of the panchayati raj representatives and funding it from various programmes which are already being implemented all over the country. There is also a need to make the training compulsory and also organise it on a continuous basis rather than making it one shot affair. This will make the panchayati raj system effective.

In the context of the role and responsibilities of the elected representatives, there are certain components which are essential for the effective functioning of the panchayati raj. These components are: knowledge, understanding and choices. The amount of knowledge required to be a good panchayati raj representative is substantial. It includes in the broad sense of the term, the physical, economic, social aspects of the village/ block and the district, knowledge of planning and financing, and also the knowledge of the panchayati raj system itself. The second component is understanding which means that the elected representative must understand his role and also the role of the officials. The understanding of the organic linkages amongst various tiers of the panchayati raj is also essential. Similarly, the component of the choices relate to information regarding various developmental programmes, their operational guidelines, procedures and the financial component, etc. These details are necessary at the time of making decisions about the training programmes. On the basis of the analyses made above, there is a need to streamline the training system and to treat training as a continuing support system. Through workshops and seminars, it should periodically inform the newly educated representatives about new development and specific problems of local self-government.

TABLES

TABLE 1
Training Programmes – 1966-67*

Description of the Training Centres (figures in brackets indicate the number of training centres)	*Categories of personnel trained (figures in brackets indicate the duration of training)*	*Number trained during the year*	*Total trained*
National Institute of Community Development (1)	(a) Senior Officials and selected non-officials like MPs and MLAs (Orientation Course) (1 month)	68	1563
	(b) Instructors at the Trg. Centres (Instructor's Course (4 1/2 months)	17	211
Orientation and Study Centres (7)	BDOs, EOs and Non-officials (General course) (2 weeks)	2264	19379**
Panchayati Raj Trg. Centres (121)	Institutional: (a) Sarpanches, Upsarpanches, & Panchayat Samiti Members (1 week) (b) Nyaya Panches & Women Members of Panchayat Samitis and Zila Parishads (10 days) (c) Part time Panchayat Secretaries and Nyaya Panchayat Secretaries (30 days)	8738***	116512***
	Peripatetic: Panches (3 days)	30688***	245074***

* Only those training programmes have been included in the table which deal with Panchayati Raj

** Includes the number trained in Orientation and Study Courses

*** Information received from 93 centres.

Source: Government of India, Department of Community Development, Report 1966-67, New Delhi, pp. 48-50.

TABLE 2
Training Programmes – 1967-68*

Description of the Training Centres (figures in brackets indicate the number of training centres)	*Categories of personnel trained (figures in brackets indicate the duration of training)*	*Number trained during the year*	*Total trained*
National Institute of Community Develop-ment (1)	(a) Senior Officials and selected non-officials like MPs and MLAs (Orientation Course) (1 month)	153	1716
	(b) Instructors at the Trg. Centres (Instructor's Course (4 1/2 months)	Information awaited from NICD	
**Composite Train-ing Centres (13)	BDOs, EOs and Non-officials and District Level officers		37831
Panchayati Raj Trg. Centres (73)	Institutional: (a) Sarpanches, Upsarpanches, & Panchayat Samiti Members (1 week) (b) Nyaya Panches & Women Members of Panchayat Samitis and Zila Parishads (10 days) (c) Part-time Panchayat Secretaries and Nyaya Panchayat Secretaries (30 days)	15802	132314
	Peripatetic: Panches (3 days)	8813	253887

* Only those training programmes have been included in the table which deal with Panchayati Raj

** In Assam and Punjab, Composite Training Centres have not been started.

Source: Government of India, Department of Community Development, Annual Report 1967-68, New Delhi, pp. 46-48.

TABLE 3
Training Programmes – 1968-69*

Description of the Training Centres (figures in brackets indicate the number of training centres)	*Categories of personnel trained (figures in brackets indicate the duration of training)*	*Number trained during the year*	*Total trained*
National Institute of Community Development	Orientation Course (7 Courses) officials, non-officials and foreigners (1 month)	157	1943
Do.	The trainers of PRTCs and foreigners (2 months)	21	21
Composite Training Centres (13)	BDOs, EOs and Non-officials district level officers (14 days)	3094	42969
Panchayati Raj Trg. Centres (55)	(a) Sarpanches, Upsarpanches, & Panchayat Samiti Members (1 week) (b) Nyaya Panches & Women Members of Panchayat Samitis and Zila Parishads (10 days) (c) Part-time Panchayat Secretary and Nyaya Panchayat Secretary (3 days) (d) Panches (3 days)		6089.63**

* Only those training programmes have been included in the table which deal with Panchayati Raj

** Includes categories of persons trained institutionally and through peripatetic teams

Source: India, Department of Community Development Report, 1968-69, New Delhi, pp.52-54.

TABLE 4
State-wise Availability of State and Lower Level Training Institutions

State	*State level institutions*				*Lower level institutions*		
	ATI	*SIRD*	*Others*	*Total*	*ETC/ VLWTC PRTC*	*FTC*	*Total*
1	*2*	*3*	*4*	*5*	*6*	*7*	*8*
Andhra Pradesh	1	1	-	2	6	12	18
Assam	1	1	-	2	9	-	9
Bihar	1	1	-	2	1	5	6
Gujarat*	1	1	-	2	10	9	19
Haryana	1	1	-	2	-	4	4
Himachal Pradesh	1	1	-	2	3	-	3
Jammu & Kashmir	1	1	-	2	-	2	2
Karnataka*	1	1	-	2	8	8	16
Kerala	1	1	1	3	6	3	9
Madhya Pradesh	1	1	-	2	8	7	15
Maharashtra*	1	1	-	2	20	4	24
Manipur*	1	1	-	2	2	-	2
Meghalaya	1	1	-	2	2	3	5
Nagaland	1	1	-	2	1	-	1
Orissa	1	1	-	2	3	6	9
Punjab	1	1	-	2	1	3	4
Rajasthan*	1	1	-	2	3	1	4
Sikkim	-	1	-	1	-	1	1
Tamil Nadu	1	1	1	3	6	8	14
Tripura*	-	1	-	1	2	1	3
Uttar Pradesh	1	1	2	4	28	17	45
West Bengal	1	1	-	2	12	8	20
Arunachal Pradesh	1	1	-	2	-	1	1
Mizoram	-	1	-	1	-	-	-
Goa, Daman & Diu	-	1	-	1	1	-	1
A&N Islands	-	-	-	-	-	-	-
Chandigarh	-	-	-	-	-	-	-
Delhi	1	-	-	1	-	1	1

1	*2*	*3*	*4*	*5*	*6*	*7*	*8*
D&N & Haveli	-	-	-	-	-	-	-
Lakshadweep	-	-	-	-	-	-	-
Pondicherry	-	-	-	-	-	1	1
All India	22	25	4	51	132	105	237

* Composite training institutes both for administrative personnel and rural development functionaries.

ATI : Administrative Training Institute

SIRD: State Institute of Rural Development

ETC: Extension Training Centre

VLWTC: Village Level Workers Training Centre

FTC: Farmers Training Centre

PRTC: Panchayat Raj Training Centre

Source:

- Training for District Planning, Report of the Study Group, Planning Commission, Government of India, New Delhi, June 1989, p. 17.
- Directory of Training Institutions in India, Training Division, Department of Personnel and Training, Ministry of Personnel, Public Grievances and Pensions. Government of India, New Delhi, October 1994, pp.91-138.
- India, Ministry of Rural Development, Annual Report 1993-94 to 1999-2000, New Delhi.

TABLE 5

Statement showing funds released for Training of Panchayati Raj Members (During the Eighth Plan Period) 1992-1997

Year	*Name of State/UT*	*Amount (In Rupees)*
1	2	3
1992-93	NIRD, Hyderabad	25,00,000.000
	Total	25,00,000.000
1993-94	LBSNAA, Mussoorie, U.P.	91,090.00
	IIPA, New Delhi	65,000.00
	KILA, Kerala	13,75,00.00
	Government of U.P.	36,00,000.00
	Government of West Bengal	29,26,000.00
	Government of Kerala	3,29,400.00
	Government of Tripura	26,45,650.00
	Total	1,10,32,140.00
1994-95	Bihar Vidyapeeth, Bihar	6,20,000.00
	Bonded Liberation Front, Delhi	1,50,000.00
	Institute of Social Sciences, New Delhi	2,90,000.00
	IGNOU (Distance Edn.Module), New Delhi	9,76,000.00
	LBSNAA, Mussoorie, U.P.	67,000.00
	Rural Litigation & Entitlement Kendra, Dehradun (UP)	1,75,000.00
	Harijan Sevak Sangh, Delhi	7,00,000.00
	IGNOU (Distance Education.Module), New Delhi	37,85,000.00
	Total	67,63,000.00
1995-96	Shanti Ashram, Coimbatore (Training), Tamil Nadu	1,63,000.00
	Mahila Chetna Manch, Bhopal (Training), Madhya Pradesh	3,22,000.00
	Centre for Research in Rural and Industrial Development, Chandigarh (Research & Training)	1,50,000.00
	LBSNAA, Mussoorie (Training), U.P.	67,000.00
	Institute of Rural Management, Anand	

1	2	3
	(Training), Gujarat	5,05,000.00
	Rural Litigation & Entitlement Kendra, Dehradun (Training), U.P.	1,75,000.00
	Government of Andhra Pradesh (Training)	50,00,000.00
	Government of Gujarat (Training)	8,82,000.00
	Government of Haryana (Training)	5,91,000.00
	Total	78,55,000.00
1996-97	Assam (Training)	16,86,300.00
	Kerala (Training Reimbursement)	83,25,000.00
	KILA (Training)	36,000.00
	Harijan Sevak Sangh (Training)	7,00,000.00
	Maharashtra (Training)	25,93,415.00
	Madhya Pradesh (Training)	28,12,050.00
	Andhra Pradesh (Training)	50,00.000.00
	Total	2,11,52,765.00
	Grand Total	4,93,02,905.00

Source: Standing Committee on Urban and Rural Development, 2002, Ministry of Rural Development, Department of Rural Development, Implementation of Part IX of the Constitution, Thirty-Seventh Report, Lok Sabha Secretariat, New Delhi, pp.220-221.

TABLE 6

Statement showing funds released for Training of Panchayati Raj: 1997-2002

(Rs. In crore)

Financial Year	*Amount allocated*	*Grants to NGOs/Institutions*	*Grants to States*
1997-1998	3.00	2.00	1.00
1998-1999	3.00	2.00	1.00
1999-2000	3.00	2.00	1.00
2000-2001	3.00	1.00	2.00
2001-2002	5.00	N.A.	N.A.
Grand Total	17.00	7.00	5.00

Source: Standing Committee on Urban and Rural Development, 2002, Ministry of Rural Development, Department of Rural Development, Implementation of Part IX of the Constitution, Thirty-Seventh Report, Lok Sabha Secretariat, New Delhi, p. 77

TABLE 6A

Statement showing funds released for Training of elected Panchayati raj representatives 2005-2006

(Rupees in crore)

Allocation	*Grants to States & NGO's*	*Grants for North-Eastern States*
24.40	19.40	5.00

Source: Annual Report 2005-2006, Ministry of Panchayati Raj, Government of India, p.18

TABLE 7
State-wise list of Panchayats and their elected Representatives as on April, 2004

S.No.	Name of State/UT	Village Panchayat (VP) No. of V.P.	No. of elected representatives Gen.	SC	ST	Women	Total
1.	Andhra Pradesh	21913	160386	31243	16662	68736	277027
2.	Arunachal Pradesh	1747	0	0	0	0	0
3.	Assam	2489	14060	782	778	7851	23471
4.	Bihar	8471	96513	18650	866	40553	156582
5.	Chhattisgarh	9139	56481	15532	52198	41913	166124
6.	Goa	190	982	0	0	457	1439
7.	Gujarat	13819	56028	9895	17290	40985	124198
8.	Haryana	6034	42800	11846	0	18356	73002
9.	Himachal Pradesh	3037	12657	4898	994	6822	25371
10.	Jharkhand	3746	0	0	0	0	0
11.	Jammu and Kashmir	2683	0	0	0	0	0
12.	Karnataka	5659	31051	14871	7499	35922	89343
13.	Kerala	991	6802	1487	169	4801	13259
14.	Madhya Pradesh	22029	119313	32585	56458	106491	314847
15.	Maharashtra	28553	118996	26824	31826	77548	255194
16.	Manipur	166	1025	38	48	611	1722
17.	Orissa	6234	49568	4930	23049	31414	118961
18.	Punjab	12445	33280	15580	0	27108	75968
19.	Rajasthan	9189	70027	24129	20126	39450	153732
20.	Sikkim	159	571	39	263	322	1195
21.	Tamil Nadu	12618	51155	19301	821	26181	97458
22.	Tripura	537	2757	876	157	1895	5685
23.	Uttar Pradesh	52028	293868	83443	207	230865	608383
24.	Uttaranchal	7227	237793	5378	703	18041	261915
25.	West Bengal	3360	22586	13645	3472	11497	51200
26.	A&N Islands	67	498	0	0	261	759
27.	Chandigarh	17	135	27	0	55	217
28.	D&N Haveli	11	4	2	118	45	169
29.	Daman & Diu	10	33	1	12	17	63
30.	Lakshadweep	10	0	0	49	30	79
31.	Pondicherry	98	0	0	0	0	0
Total:		234676	1479369	346002	233765	838227	2897363

(Contd...)

S.No.	Name of State/UT	Intermediate Panchayat (IP)					
		No. of I.P.	No. of elected representatives				
			Gen.	SC	ST	Women	Total
1.	Andhra Pradesh	1095	10938	2586	1093	4919	19536
2.	Arunachal Pradesh	150	0	0	0	0	0
3.	Assam	203	1236	80	86	746	2148
4.	Bihar	531	9661	1859	91	4065	15676
5.	Chhattisgarh	146	1259	318	1062	906	3545
6.	Goa	0	0	0	0	0	0
7.	Gujarat	225	1953	265	550	1393	4161
8.	Haryana	114	1879	551		842	3272
9.	Himachal Pradesh	75	1108	437	113	562	2220
10.	Jharkhand	211	0	0	0	0	0
11.	Jammu and Kashmir	0	0	0	0	0	0
12.	Karnataka	175	1335	583	244	1375	3537
13.	Kerala	152	803	188	18	629	1638
14.	Madhya Pradesh	313	2476	682	1139	2159	6456
15.	Maharashtra	349	1902	447	528	1407	4284
16.	Manipur	0	0	0	0	0	0
17.	Orissa	314	3498	1025	1704	2188	8415
18.	Punjab	140	1141	526		813	2480
19.	Rajasthan	237	3434	968	855	1908	7165
20.	Sikkim	0	0	0	0	0	0
21.	Tamil Nadu	385	3384	1369	47	1770	6570
22.	Tripura	23	100	78	15	106	299
23.	Uttar Pradesh	813	25530	7743	17	18580	51870
24.	Uttaranchal	95	1807	241	44	1133	3225
25.	West Bengal	333	3669	2383	604	1923	8579
26.	A&N Islands	7	42	0	0	25	67
27.	Chandigarh	1	11	4	0	6	21
28.	D&N Haveli	0	0	0	0	0	0
29.	Daman & Diu	0	0	0	0	0	0
30.	Lakshadweep	0	0	0	0	0	0
31.	Pondicherry	10	0	0	0	0	0
Total:		6097	77166	22333	8210	47455	155164

(Contd...)

S.No.	Name of State/UT	District Panchayat (DP)					
		No. of D.P.	No. of elected representatives				
			Gen.	SC	ST	Women	Total
1.	Andhra Pradesh	22	812	196	87	364	1459
2.	Arunachal Pradesh	15	0	0	0	0	0
3.	Assam	20	236	19	18	117	390
4.	Bihar	38	966	187	9	410	1572
5.	Chhattisgarh	16	152	30	112	95	389
6.	Goa	2	33	0	0	17	50
7.	Gujarat	25	390	39	115	275	819
8.	Haryana	19	247	67	0	109	423
9.	Himachal Pradesh	12	165	65	21	87	338
10.	Jharkhand	22	0	0	0	0	0
11.	Jammu and Kashmir	0	0	0	0	0	0
12.	Karnataka	27	379	158	54	339	930
13.	Kerala	14	165	33	4	105	307
14.	Madhya Pradesh	45	286	78	122	248	734
15.	Maharashtra	33	931	225	267	658	2081
16.	Manipur	4	36	1	2	22	61
17.	Orissa	30	496	139	219	296	1150
18.	Punjab	17	130	60	0	89	279
19.	Rajasthan	32	653	191	164	364	1372
20.	Sikkim	4	50	6	36	29	121
21.	Tamil Nadu	29	341	139	3	173	656
22.	Tripura	4	28	22	4	28	82
23.	Uttar Pradesh	71	1025	313	0	788	2126
24.	Uttaranchal	13	193	28	5	119	345
25.	West Bengal	18	314	202	51	156	723
26.	A&N Islands	1	20	0	0	10	30
27.	Chandigarh	1	7	3	0	3	13
28.	D&N Haveli	1	0	0	12	4	16
29.	Daman & Diu	1	12	0	3	10	25
30.	Lakshadweep	1	0	0	14	8	22
31.	Pondicherry	0	0	0	0	0	0
Total:		537	8067	2201	1322	4923	16513

Grand Total:(VP) 2897363 + (IP) 155164 + (DP) 16513 = 3069040

(Contd...)

Meghalaya, Mizoram and Nagaland have traditional councils.

NCT of Delhi – Panchayati Raj system is yet to be revived.

0 = Information not available

Jharkhand - Elections to the local bodies are yet to be conducted

Jammu & Kashmir – Has not adopted the Constitution (Seventy-Third) Amendment Act, 1992

Arunachal Pradesh – Panchahat Elections held on 2.4.03 except in Tirap District

Manipur, Sikkim, Dadar and Nagar Haveli, Daman and Diu, and Lakshadweep – Intermediate Panchayat does not exist.

Source: Ministry of Rural Development, Government of India, New Delhi, April, 2004.

TABLE 8
Number of Educational Institutions

S.No. States/UTs	Univer sity	Arts, Science & Commerce Colleges	Teacher Training Colleges	Jr. Colleges/ Hr. Sec Schools	High/ Post Basic Schools
1. Andhra Pradesh	19	998	87	2334	10277
2. Arunachal Pradesh	1	7	0	68	116
3. Assam	5	280	28	684	4069
4. Bihar	15	742	15	780	4228
5. Goa	1	20	2	81	355
6. Gujarat	10	422	42	2051	4292
7. Haryana	4	150	20	1208	3020
8. Himachal Pradesh	3	65	1	649	1183
9. Jammu & Kashmir	3	33	4	274	1237
10. Karnataka	13	916	66	1857	8353
11. Kerala	7	186	19	1406	2776
12. Madhya Pradesh	18	413	20	5155	5044
13. Maharashtra	18	873	251	3650	11687
14. Manipur	2	50	3	76	529
15. Meghalaya	1	33	2	40	532
16. Mizoram	0	30	1	30	383
17. Nagaland	1	33	2	23	315
18. Orissa	8	567	13	1031	6165
19. Punjab	5	204	22	1189	2199
20. Rajasthan	7	267	45	2165	4544
21. Sikkim	1	2	1	33	77
22. Tamil Nadu	15	426	22	3439	4500
23. Tripura	1	14	1	226	403
24. Uttar Pradesh	22	758	121	6078	3837
25. West Bengal	11	350	32	2516	6882
26. A&N Islands	0	2	1	48	44
27. Chandigarh	1	12	2	49	56
28. D&N Haveli	0	0	0	6	10
29. Daman & Diu	0	1	1	5	20
30. Delhi	5	64	6	1149	405
31. Lakshadweep	0	0	0	6	9
32. Pondicherry	1	8	4	66	128
India	198	7926	834	38372	87675

Source: India. Department of Secondary and Higher Education, Ministry of Human Resource Development, Selected Educational Statistics, 2000-2001, New Delhi, 2002, pp.9-10.

Entries in the table have been taken selectively.

TABLE 9
Number of Teachers – Higher Secondary School/Junior Colleges

S.No. States/UTs	Number of Teachers			% of trained teachers	Number of Female Teachers per 100 Male Teachers
	Men	Women	Total		
1	2	3	4	5	6
1. Andhra Pradesh	21428	8085	29513	95	38
2. Arunachal Pradesh	1454	350	1804	61	24
3. Assam	15450	6147	21597	50	40
4. Bihar	4375	1882	6257	95	43
5. Goa	737	697	1434	85	95
6. Gujarat	27926	9976	37902	99	36
7. Haryana	14944	13393	28337	98	90
8. Himachal Pradesh	8106	4052	12158	100	50
9. Jammu and Kashmir	5071	2663	7734	48	53
10. Karnataka	19475	5005	24480	20	26
11. Kerala	5097	9540	14637	98	187
12. Madhya Pradesh	43675	21577	65252	75	49
13. Maharashtra	74606	29433	104039	99	39
14. Manipur	1273	855	2128	47	67
15. Meghalaya	366	382	748	98	104
16. Mizoram	239	231	470	34	97
17. Nagaland	427	395	822	21	93
18. Orissa	7361	2263	9624	100	31
19. Punjab	14750	19059	33809	99	129
20. Rajasthan	30729	13024	43753	95	42
21. Sikkim	731	326	1057	51	45
22. Tamil Nadu	78136	19833	97969	100	25
23. Tripura	5607	2649	8256	49	47
24. Uttar Pradesh	89473	21143	110616	97	24
25. West Bengal	41582	14662	56244	84	35
26. A&N Islands	986	917	1903	98	93
27. Chandigarh	645	1782	2427	100	276

(Contd....)

1	*2*	*3*	*4*	*5*	*6*
28. D&N Haveli	37	71	158	100	82
29. Daman and Diu	44	16	60	100	36
30. Delhi	14507	13368	27875	100	92
31. Lakshadweep	45	3	48	100	7
32. Pondicherry	1346	1341	2687	100	100
India	530678	225120	755798	90	42

Source: India. Department of Secondary and Higher Education, Ministry of Human Resource Development, Selected Educational Statistics, 2001-2002, New Delhi, 2000 , p.57. (Entries in the table have been taken selectively)

TABLE 10
Number of Teachers – High Schools/ Post Basic Schools

S.No. States/UTs	Number of Teachers Men	Women	Total	% of trained teachers	Number of Female Teachers per 100 Male Teachers
1	2	3	4	5	6
1. Andhra Pradesh	74841	56483	131324	92	75
2. Arunachal Pradesh	1425	422	1847	45	30
3. Assam	35017	12476	47493	30	36
4. Bihar	37863	4812	42675	95	13
5. Goa	2501	3986	6487	97	159
6. Gujarat	20593	5581	26174	99	27
7. Haryana	17906	11343	29249	96	63
8. Himachal Pradesh	6934	3392	10326	100	49
9. Jammu and Kashmir	13863	6531	20394	57	47
10. Karnataka	52517	26731	79248	100	51
11. Kerala	31774	63513	95287	100	200
12. Madhya Pradesh	21561	10249	31810	68	48
13. Maharashtra	98247	46759	145006	98	48
14. Manipur	5538	3324	8862	28	60
15. Meghalaya	2468	2421	4889	36	98
16. Mizoram	2219	661	2880	50	30
17. Nagaland	3206	2622	5828	45	82
18. Orissa	40630	10940	51570	100	27
19. Punjab	14551	15991	30542	99	110
20. Rajasthan	36989	12618	49607	89	34
21. Sikkim	946	585	1531	44	62
22. Tamil Nadu	35981	15119	51100	100	42
23. Tripura	6773	2841	9614	32	42
24. Uttar Pradesh	26059	6064	32123	97	23
25. West Bengal	57789	19888	77677	86	34
26. A&N Islands	435	417	852	100	96
27. Chandigarh	445	2264	2709	100	509

(Contd....)

1	2	3	4	5	6
28. D&N Haveli	33	14	47	99	42
29. Daman and Diu	166	98	264	100	59
30. Delhi	2901	2806	5707	100	97
31. Lakshadweep	320	100	420	100	31
32. Pondicherry	1069	1234	2303	95	115
India	653560	352285	1005845	89	54

Source: India. Department of Secondary and Higher Education, Ministry of Human Resource Development, Selected Educational Statistics, 2001-2002, New Delhi, 2002, p.58. (Entries in the table have been taken selectively)

TABLE 11

Plan Outlay for Annual Plan 2000-2001 for the schemes/ programmes of the Central Ministries under the subject mentioned in Eleventh Schedule of Constitution

(Rs. In crore)

S.No.	*Name of the Scheme/Programme*	*Outlay* 2000-2001
1.	Crop Husbandry	1380.22
2.	Soil and Water Conservation	63.42
3.	Animal Husbandry	77.07
4.	Dairy Development	36.45
5.	Fisheries	16.61
6.	Forestry and Wildlife	281.65
7.	Plantations	169.35
8.	Agricultural Research and Education	550.00
9.	Agricultural Financial Institutions	28.76
10.	Other Agricultural Programmes	6.67
11.	Land Reforms	67.50
12.	Minor Irrigation	88.67
13.	Non-Conventional Sources of Energy	858.46
14.	Village and Small Industries	1125.35
15.	Road and Bridges	5548.15
16.	General Education	4433.06
17.	Technical Education	496.18
18.	Family Welfare	3200.00
19.	Water Supply and Sanitation	2071.03
20.	Housing	3869.73
21.	Welfare of SC, ST and OBCs	997.74
22.	Social Security and Welfare	2231.85
23.	Nutrition	2.90
24.	Other Social Services	1.20
25.	Special Programme for Rural Development	1075.45
26.	Rural Employment	2798.40
	Total:	31575.87

Source: Standing Committee on Urban and Rural Development 2002, Ministry of Rural Development, Department of Rural Development, Implementation of Part IX of the Constitution, Thirty-Seventh Report, Lok Sabha Secretariat, New Delhi, pp.208-209.

TABLE 11A

Plan Outlay for Annual Plan 2000-2001 for the schemes/ programmes of the State Plan of the State Governments under the subject mentioned in Eleventh Schedule of Constitution

(Rs. In crore)

S.No.	*Name of the Scheme/Programme*	*Outlay* 2000-2001
1.	Crop Husbandry	1268.77
2.	Soil and Water Conservation	64350
3.	Animal Husbandry	354.19
4.	Dairy Development	49.87
5.	Fisheries	205.95
6.	Forestry and Wildlife	1393.03
7.	Plantations	4.63
8.	Agricultural Research and Education	292.21
9.	Agricultural Financial Institutions	61.63
10.	Other Agricultural Programmes	9818
11.	IRDP & Allied Programme	516.16
12.	NREP/JRY	116122
13.	Other Programme like EAS etc.	106246
14.	Land Reforms	294.08
15.	Minor Irrigation	1907.93
16.	Non-Conventional Sources of Energy	119.43
17.	Village and Small Industries	800.87
18.	Road and Bridges	8128.44
19.	Road Transport	1265.30
20.	Inland Water Transport	16.74
21.	Other Transport Services	614.50
22.	General Education	4972.07
23.	Technical Education	422.49
24.	Art and Culture	171.07
25.	Medical and Public Health	3306.64
26.	Water Supply and Sanitation	6031.74
27.	Housing	1936.57
28.	Welfare of SCs, STs and OBCs	1972.99
29.	Social Welfare	904.26
30.	Nutrition	721.79
31.	Other Social Services	119.86
	Total:	40818.65

Source: Standing Committee on Urban and Rural Development 2002, Ministry of Rural Development, Department of Rural Development, Implementation of Part IX of the Constitution, Thirty-Seventh Report, Lok Sabha Secretariat, New Delhi, pp.210-211.

TABLE 12

Grants-in-aid for the panchayats as recommended by the Twelfth Finance Commission to augment the consolidated fund of the states for the period 2005-2010

Sl. No.	*State*	*Panchayats*	
		Per cent	*(Rs. Crore)*
1.	Andhra Pradesh	7.935	1587
2.	Arunachal Pradesh	0.340	68
3.	Assam	2.630	526
4.	Bihar	8.120	1624
5.	Chhattisgarh	3.075	615
6.	Goa	0.090	18
7.	Gujarat	4.655	931
8.	Haryana	1.940	388
9.	Himachal Pradesh	0.735	147
10.	Jammu & Kashmir	1.405	281
11.	Jharkhand	2.410	482
12.	Karnataka	4.440	888
13.	Kerala	4.925	985
14.	Madhya Pradesh	8.315	1663
15.	Maharashtra	9.915	1983
16.	Manipur	0.230	46
17.	Meghalaya	0.250	50
18.	Mizoram	0.100	20
19.	Nagaland	0.200	40
20.	Orissa	4.015	803
21.	Punjab	1.620	324
22.	Rajasthan	6.150	1230
23.	Sikkim	0.065	13
24.	Tamil Nadu	4.350	870
25.	Tripura	0.285	57
26.	Uttar Pradesh	14.640	2928
27.	Uttaranchal	0.810	162
28.	West Bengal	6.355	1271
	Total:	100.000	20000

Source: The State of the Panchayats – A Mid-Term Review and Appraisal, 22 November 2006, Vol.III, Ministry of Panchayati Raj, Government of India, pp. 281-282.

TABLE 13
Schedule – XI

1. Agriculture, including agricultural extension.
2. Land improvement, implementation of land reforms, lands consolidation and soil conservation.
3. Minor irrigation, Water management and Watershed Development.
4. Animal husbandry, dairying and poultry.
5. Fisheries.
6. Social forestry and farm forestry.
7. Minor forest produce.
8. Small scale industries, including food-processing industries.
9. Khadi, village and cottage industries.
10. Rural housing.
11. Drinking water.
12. Fuel and fodder.
13. Roads, culverts, bridges, ferries, waterways and other means of communication.
14. Rural electrification, including distribution of electricity.
15. Non-conventional energy sources.
16. Poverty alleviation programmes.
17. Education, including primary and secondary schools.
18. Technical training and vocational education.
19. Adult and non-formal education.
20. Libraries.
21. Cultural activities.
22. Markets and fairs.
23. Health and sanitation, including hospitals, primary health centres and dispensaries.
24. Family welfare.
25. Women and Child development.
26. Social Welfare, including welfare of the handicapped and mentally retarded.
27. Welfare of the weaker sections, and in particular of the Scheduled Castes and Scheduled Tribes.
28. Public distribution system.
29. Maintenance of community assets.

Sources: Standing Committee on Urban and Rural Development 2002, Ministry of Rural Development, Department of Rural Development, Implementation of Part IX of the Constitution, Thirty-Seventh Report, Lok Sabha Secretariat, New Delhi, pp.109-110.

Index